Journey to the Manger
with St. Patrick & Friends

A SIX-WEEK
CELTIC ADVENT DEVOTIONAL

Jean McLachlan Hess

ISBN-13: 978-1492830931

DEDICATION

To my mother, Jeanne Fisher McLachlan.
Your sacrificial love and your faith in God continue to inspire me
everyday.

CONTENTS

ACKNOWLEDGMENTS

The positive impact of a Six-Week Celtic Advent in my personal life sowed thoughts of taking this new, yet ancient, tradition and offering it afresh to God's people. Bringing these thoughts to reality began a wonderful journey accompanied by wonderful people.

Peggy McIntyre, Patti Crowley, Mary Hanson, Rick Hess, and Marjory Vawter all had a role in editing, teaching, and encouraging me. Thank you.

I owe a debt of thanks to my family. Rick, you never wavered in your faithful love even in the times when I became more than a little crazy. Fraser, thank you for your technical knowledge, your wisdom, and your patience. Greig, you created a cover that took my breath away. It still does. Thank you. Jenna, Elizabeth, Fiona, and David, thank you for your grace.

To our 316 (three siks-teen) church family: your belief in this book and in the benefits of a Celtic Advent helped me keep my eyes on the finish line.

Heartfelt thanks to Dr. Gordon MacDonald. Gordon and Gayle, you graciously worked though each of these devotions on a personal level. Your support and Gordon's foreword have inspired me to keep writing.

Without the sense of God's call to write this book, His constant presence and His reassuring words, "I've got this, Jean," I suspect I would never have completed this work.

My utmost thanks goes to Emmanuel. Knowing that He was and is and will always be "with me" is the rock solid foundation on which I have written each word.

FOREWORD

In praise of *Journey to the Manger*
with St. Patrick & Friends

You have in your hands a delightful piece of reflective Christian literature. It has been assembled by a remarkably cheerful and insightful woman, a friend, Jean McLachlan Hess. Having been highly influenced by the Celtic tradition of Christian faith, Jean has provided us with some fresh new ways to look at and experience the Advent season—the time when we refresh our worship of the Christ who entered the world as a baby and spoke to us the words of life.

When the last weeks of each year come at us, we always face a choice. Will we be captured by the famed *Christmas Season* (replete with commercialism, religious pageantry, and football bowls), or will we celebrate Advent—a time of renewing one's self, one's spiritual community, one's walk with God.

Leave Jean Hess's book alone if you chose the first—the so-called *Christmas Season*. But seize her book and drain it for everything it has to offer should you choose the second—that which for centuries has been called *Advent*.

Although I have loved reading of St. Patrick, his followers and their efforts to evangelize Ireland, I could not claim to be a scholar of the Celtic tradition of the Christian faith. But I have been greatly wooed by the Celtic prayers, the Celtic appreciation of the beauty of God and His creation, the vigor of the Celtic worship experience which braces people to live in a real world with all of its daily challenges. Let me say it boldly: Celtic Christianity is not for the fainthearted, nor for those seeking a cloistered, diluted kind of faith.

Perhaps I go over the top in saying this, but I find the Celtic tradition perfectly fit for the twenty-first century, and I find myself wondering if—as the years of this century pass by—we will not see a younger generation rush after Patrick and his ways and find all they seek in his spiritual legacy.

Jean Hess has taken a look at that segment of the Christian calendar called Advent and suggested that we observe it in the spirit of the Celtic Christians. In so doing, she calls for us to light seven (not the traditional five) candles, one for each week of the Advent period. In addition to the normal five (hope, peace, joy, love, Christ), she suggests two more: a God candle and a Holy Spirit candle.

This, I think, is a worthy idea.

Jean's intention "is designed to take us from the insane stress and busyness of the weeks before Christmas to a calmer and less harried pace. It is designed to invite Emmanuel to travel with us on our journey to the Manger. It is designed to invite Emmanuel to be our navigator through the smooth and rough terrain of this season."

I draw Jean Hess's words into my soul, and they provide a relaxation of spirit. Too often I have been one of those who has finished the *Christmas Season* saying to anyone who might listen, "I'll never go through a Christmas like that again." It's my standard complaint about a time of the year which has been hijacked by the merchants, the athletes, even, sadly, the Christian promoters who can think of a hundred ways to siphon off our energy for everything but a simple welcoming of Jesus, as the Christ child, back into our lives.

Should you choose to follow Jean through the Advent weeks, lighting candles as you go along, you'll find a set of uplifting and deepening reflections for every day. They are not burdensome or time-consuming.

But you may need an altar, a small unpretentious place in your home where you can meet and hear God's voice. The altar can be a small table with a Bible or sacred picture. It can be a bench under a tree (if you live in warm weather). Wherever your altar may be, go to it daily and spend a few minutes in the divine presence.

This is where Jean Hess's book, *Journey to the Manger with St. Patrick & Friends*, becomes of value. Each reading is designed to help us center our thoughts upon the true thrust of Advent. The mind is concentrated; the heart is centered; the body is relaxed.

In this book there are rousing Celtic prayers:

I bind unto myself the name,
The strong name of the Trinity,
By invocation of the same,
The Three in One and One in Three . . . .

There are wonderful stories: "I was five years old," Jean writes, "and Christmas was coming." You can't imagine what comes next as Jean reminisces on the generosity of God as understood through the eyes of a child.

There are old hymns: "Will your anchor hold in the storms of life, when the clouds unfold their wings of strife. . . ."

Great Psalms . . . encouraging promises . . . poems from the heart of the great mothers and fathers of the Christian movement.

There are reminders, challenges, gentle rebukes, assurances of the love of Jesus.

This is a wonderful book, and, having gone through it once, I fully intend to make a second journey through it when the next Advent season comes again.

A word to those unfamiliar with the Celtic Christian tradition. Much of its flavor arose in the time when Christianity was all but dead on the European Continent. One wonders what would have happened to the Christian witness in the world had it not been for the Celtic Christians of the fifth through ninth centuries, who kept the flame of faith alive and faithfully proclaimed the Word of God.

Their Celtic ways may not always be our ways. But what this bold people, mostly Irish, left us as a legacy is simply stirring and brilliant. How can one avoid an arousal of the heart when he/she reads words attributed to one ancient Celtic Christian:

> I will kindle my fire this morning
> In the presence of the holy angels of heaven
> Without malice, without jealousy, without envy,
> But the Holy Son of God to shield me.
>
> God, kindle Thou in my heart within
> A flame of love to my neighbor,
> To my foe, to my friend, to my kindred-all.

In giving us this spiritual guide for Advent, Jean Hess has provided us a wonderful gift. I am among those who are truly grateful.

Gordon MacDonald

Chancellor, Denver Seminary

INTRODUCTION

What does it take to make a memorable Celtic Advent? Most experts would recommend using only the finest ingredients and following a professionally endorsed recipe, one that has stood the test of time and will secure optimal results. My favorite Advent recipe meets all of these requirements. It's a "family" recipe, passed down through more generations than I care to count. This recipe has been modified over the centuries, and this latest version should more or less guarantee that your Christmas will be filled with the fragrance of spiritual richness.

Celtic Advent Recipe

Ingredients:

AD Fourth Century

Roman and local Gaul customs

4 secret ingredients

6-week Lenten fast

1 cup of Preparation

Joyful Anticipation

November and December

1 ton of Hope

1 ton of Peace

1 ton of Joy

1 ton of Love

Christ

Directions:

Take a measure of the fourth century and combine this with one handful of Roman customs and two handfuls of the customs of Gaul. Since Gaul has become our modern day France, you may want to add a little Oo-La-La for extra flavor.

In the early days one was instructed to marinate these ingredients until you added six weeks of Lenten fast. Set your timer for November 15, and then let this mixture rest, stirring it daily until December 24.

Through the Middle Ages it became common to mix in a cup of preparation for the Second Coming of Christ. Eventually people preferred the taste that adding joyful anticipation produced. This new ingredient replaced the Lenten fasting. As this Celtic Advent recipe continued to change, four new ingredients were added. These were hope, peace, joy, and love. These additions changed the flavor of this season drastically; therefore it was received with great enthusiasm. Unfortunately, this cut the marinating time by two weeks. Six weeks became the four Sundays before Christmas. As eagerly as many received this change, it did not enhance the overall benefits of what constitutes a Celtic Advent. In fact, some versions of the recipe dropped the term *Celtic* all together. This shortened time and the new name *Advent* became more popular.

I suspect the later generations, then and now, had no idea just how much they were missing.

To counter this deficit, and for optimum success and delight, I wholeheartedly endorse adding back in the hush-hush ingredients. These remained a family secret for generations, but, in my opinion, the time has come to share them with the world. What are these secret ingredients? Come closer and I will tell you. The first of these is "one group of Celtic monks." When you use this ingredient, you enhance this recipe exponentially. Not only does this reintroduce the original marinating time of six weeks, it also adds four additional days. It does this by bringing with it the second secret ingredient.

"What is it?" you ask. This is a very ancient and effusive ingredient. It produces such a powerful aroma, you may be tempted to take time out to dwell in the moment and enjoy the experience. This ingredient, which was introduced by our group of Celtic monks, is the Feast of Martin of Tours. These two ingredients take us back to a Celtic Advent and then take it to a whole new level. First of all the marinating time begins November 11. Secondly, the broad-brush strokes of Martin's life story make us aware that his love and service to Christ add a deep richness to the end result.

The most recent upgrade to this ancient recipe includes a personal addition. In our time, we mark Advent by the use of designated candles that reflect the ingredients of hope, peace, joy, and love. A question arises: What will represent the two extra weeks? The answer: two more candles.

More candles? Yes, therefore we need extra ingredients. My two secret ingredients take this recipe from a well-balanced Advent meal to a Celtic Advent banquet for the soul.

I hear you ask, "What are these two new ingredients?" The answer is simple yet profound and reflects *who* rather than what. They are none other than God and the Holy Spirit.

The whole intention of Advent is to lead us to the Christ Child. The whole intention of my Celtic Advent Recipe is to lead us to the Christ Child by way of the Father and the Holy Spirit. In Celtic Christianity all three persons of the Trinity were important. You do not find them separated, one from the other. Neither do you find one elevated over the other. Therefore, our recipe is made perfect by adding these two final ingredients. I have been following this recipe for the past few years, and my experience of Christmas has been richer than ever before.

The Celtic Advent is designed to invite Emmanuel to travel with us on our journey to the Manger. It is designed to invite Emmanuel to be our navigator through the smooth and rough terrain of this season. It is designed to invite Emmanuel to impart His vision to us individually, that we may reach our destination renewed and focused on Him.

All the ingredients for this recipe are found within the pages of this book. Are you ready to make a wonderful Celtic Advent for yourself and for others? I look forward to seeing you at the Manger.

I am the LORD, and there is no other; apart from me there is no God. I will strengthen you, though you have not acknowledged me.

ISAIAH 45:5

In Scotland, on the beautiful island of Iona, you will find the ancient high-standing stone cross of St. Martin. St. Martin? Why not St. Patrick or St. Columba? Isn't Iona one the most sacred Celtic Christian sites? If so, then how did a man named Martin, born in Hungary around AD 316, ever become connected to and revered by Celtic Christians? And how is he the one to whom the observance of the season of Advent can be traced?

St. Martin of Tours, as he came to be known, was originally given the name Mars, after the god of war. His parents had no interest in Christianity. Yet at the age of ten, Martin secretly entered a church and asked that they receive him as a *catechumen*, a pupil. When he turned twelve, he desired baptism, but his parents forbade it. Martin's father, a senior officer in the Roman Army, forced Martin into the military at the age of fifteen.

While stationed at Gaul (modern-day France), tradition tells us Martin saw a beggar at the gates of the city. The sight of this nearly naked man pierced Martin's heart. In response he took his sword and cut his cloak in two, giving half to the beggar. That night Martin had a dream. In the dream he saw Jesus wearing the half-cloak he had given to the beggar. He heard Jesus say to the angels, "Here is Martin, the unbaptized Roman soldier. He has clad me." The dream confirmed the call of God on Martin's life. He received baptism at age eighteen.

Leaving the army proved difficult for Martin but his call to follow Christ compelled him to find a way out. Martin became a monk and went on to serve God faithfully. In 371 he became Bishop of Tours. The people of Tours, a prominently pagan diocese, slowly gravitated to his teaching. Martin's compassion for children and the poor won many hearts for the Kingdom of God.

It is believed that Martin died on November 8, 397. He had requested to be buried in the Cemetery of the Poor. This took place on November 11th. Martin left a rich legacy for those who followed after him. Tradition tells us that from the late 4th Century to the Middle Ages, much of Western Europe, including Great Britain, entered into a forty day fast beginning on November 11th. It was called "the forty days of St. Martin." The evening before the fast, in celebration of his life, the Feast of St. Martin took place. This feast is still celebrated in many European countries. The period of fasting was later shortened and called "Advent" by the Church.

At an early age Martin had desired something more than his pagan life, but it seemed impossible: he had to follow in his father's footsteps. His desire for a Christian life could have ended there. Although Martin had not yet fully acknowledged God, God had not forgotten him. And God does not forget anyone. He longs for all to be saved.

Martin endured strong opposition in His life, especially with regard to his becoming a Christian. How did he overcome the obstacles? I suspect that those who encountered the ten-year old Martin, when he first desired to know more about faith in Christ, continued in prayer for him long after circumstances forced him to step away from his desired journey. God delights not only to hear the prayers of His people, but He also delights to answer them. Praying for the lost fills our heavenly Father's heart with joy.

We all have people in our families and in our circle of friends who have not yet acknowledged God. We may have prayed for certain people for a long time and felt that they would never come to know Christ. Martin's story encourages us to keep praying. God's timing is perfect. The prayers of God's people have power and Martin's life testifies to this truth.

Oh, you want to know the connection between Martin and Iona? The answer is St. Patrick. Patrick is believed to have been Martin's grandnephew. Before Patrick returned to Ireland he went to Gaul (modern day France), studied there and then carried out several years of ministry in the style and footsteps of his granduncle Martin. Out of Patrick's ministry in Ireland came the ministry of St. Columba and it was Columba whose greatest ministry had its base on Iona. Small world, isn't it?

Ponder:

Think back to your own journey to faith in God and belief in Jesus Christ. Which people in your life prayed you into the Kingdom?

Dwell:

God did not wait for us to have our lives together before He drew us, by His loving-kindness, into His Kingdom. Spend a few minutes meditating on the knowledge that it was "while we were yet sinners, Christ died for us" (Romans 5:8 KJV). Praise Him for His mercy and grace.

Action:

Give thanks for the people who prayed you into the Kingdom.

As you journey through Advent to welcome the Christ child, pray for those you know who have yet to receive Jesus as Savior and Lord.

.

Week One
Light the **GOD** Candle

God
is our refuge and strength,
an ever-present help in trouble.
Psalm 46:1

Do not be anxious about anything, but in everything, by prayer and petition, with thanksgiving, present your requests to God.

PHILIPPIANS 4:6

Prayer was the heartbeat of the early Celtic Christians. They prayed about most, if not all, aspects of their daily life: from the weaver at the loom and the farmer sowing the seeds, right through to the fisherman, the milkmaid, and the crofter. When she arose in the morning to stoke the embers of the previous night's fire, the woman would pray:

I will kindle my fire this morning
In the presence of the holy angels of heaven
Without malice, without jealousy, without envy,
But the Holy Son of God to shield me.

God, kindle Thou in my heart within
A flame of love to my neighbor,
To my foe, to my friend, to my kindred all.

Several types of prayer held special prominence: Trinitarian Prayer (prayers that included the Father, Son, and Holy Spirit); praying the Scriptures; creation praise and prayer; Lorica Prayers.

Celtic Christians called prayers for protection Lorica Prayers. The most famous is St. Patrick's Breastplate. From the outset, Patrick engaged in spiritual warfare. If he had any chance of winning Ireland for Christ, he knew it would not come through any power of his own. Patrick became a man of God and a mighty man of prayer. The following two stanzas from Patrick's Breastplate give insight into the daily battle the Celts faced:

Against the demon snares of sin, the vice that gives temptation force,
The natural lusts that war within, the hostile men that mar my course;
Or few or many, far or nigh, in every place and in all hours,
Against the fierce hostility, I bind to me these holy powers.

Against all Satan's spells and wiles, against false words of heresy,
Against the knowledge that defiles, against the heart's idolatry,
Against the wizard's evil craft, against the death wound and the burning,
The choking wave and the poisoned shaft, protect me, Christ, till Thy returning.

God longs for us to bring our concerns, large and small to Him. He desires to carry the load we bear. Are we ready to let him?

Ponder:

Why do I continue to hang on to heavy burdens when I could give them to the One who can and does deal powerfully with them?

Dwell:

Jesus said, "Come to me, all you who are weary and burdened, and I will give you rest. Take my yoke upon you and learn from me, for I am gentle and humble in heart, and you will find rest for your souls. For my yoke is easy and my burden is light" (Matthew 11:28-30).

Action:

Do you wait until you are at the end of your rope before you cry out to God? Imagine yourself carrying a heavy bag full of rocks. Visualize God standing next to you, offering to take your bag and carry it for you. If you are not ready to give Him everything, He will take whatever you are willing to part with.

God I give you:

1.

2.

3.

Comfort, comfort my people, says your God.

ISAIAH 40:1

For many people the Christmas season can become one of the most painful times of the year, especially if we do not have family near. It can even become a burden *because* family is near. Family breakdowns can make Christmas seem anything but the "hap-happiest" time of the year. Separation or divorce has the power to totally strip this season of joy and peace. The same difficulties can arise when we have lost a loved one. The empty place at the table or in our hearts can make us wish the season would just disappear. In the midst of our sadness and pain, God says to us, "Comfort, comfort my people."

I experienced this deep sense of comfort last year when my sister, Sylvia, died. She lived in Australia, and earlier in the year when I received the news that she had grown very ill, my daughter and I visited with her for three weeks. I saw her faith in God grow during this difficult time. I planned to return and spend time with her before she died.

Five months later, I received a text to say that little time remained. That evening I was working on a talk to present the following night to the Enlighten Foundation. Every part of my being longed to be with my sister and to comfort her, but what did God want from me? I wept almost all of the next day. Should I keep my commitment to speak, or should I take the evening flight to Australia? My family prayed for me and with me and, in the end, I felt God tell me to stay in Denver and keep my commitment to speak.

I did speak, miraculously without crying. The God of all comfort was with me and I felt Him fill me with His peace. Sylvia passed thirty-six hours after I received the text. I would not have made it in time to be with her, even if I had left when I received the news.

At the time, only two people in the Enlighten Foundation knew of my dilemma. A few days later, Anne, the Founder and CEO, called me. She had attended my presentation but had only just learned of my story. She called to thank me and to pass on words of comfort and encouragement. Then she shared something that brought further consolation to me. In my presentation I briefly mentioned Celtic Advent and my plan to walk that path. Anne informed me that she would like to purchase a Celtic Advent wreath for me and dedicate it to the memory of my sister Sylvia.

This beautiful pewter wreath, complete with Celtic ornate knotting provides another measure of God's comfort to me. This precious gift drew me into the deep meaning of the manger and led me through a journey to the richest Christmas I have ever experienced.

Praise be to the God and Father of our Lord Jesus Christ,
the Father of compassion and the God of all comfort.

2 CORINTHIANS 1:3

Ponder:

Think back to times in your life when you were overwhelmed with grief or sorrow and remember how you experienced God's comfort.

Dwell:

When sadness overwhelms us, God weeps with us. He collects our tears in jars. He scoops us into His loving arms and holds us to Himself.

Action:

Is this Christmas season going to be a painful one for you? Share your pain and struggle with Him. Invite Him and His comfort into your grief.

You may know someone who will have a difficult Christmas season this year. Ask God to show you how you can serve Him as an agent of His comfort and love in their life.

Be strong and courageous. Do not be afraid or terrified because of them,
for the LORD your God goes with you;
he will never leave you nor forsake you.

DEUTERONOMY 31:6

Several years ago, when God placed a call on my life to research and embrace Celtic Christianity, excitement rose up within me. My husband and I had sought God's plan and design for our church. God's answer: Celtic Christianity. Celtic formed part of my DNA. Born and raised in Scotland, I had never given much thought to my heritage. I had no idea that this journey into things Celtic would revolutionize my life and transform my relationship with Christ.

The Celts were *peregrine*—people of the journey. They never worried about where they were going or how they would get there, because they knew that God would lead the way. They trusted His promise to be with them, to never leave them nor forsake them; He always proved faithful.

As I studied the lives and ministries of these ancient Celtic saints, I became enthralled by their love of the Word, the depth of their prayer life, and the way they experienced God: Father, Son, and Holy Spirit. They had an expectation of encountering their maker in all things, at all times, and in all places. They lived an *Emmanuel—God with us* life, as the normal way to follow their Lord.

This *Emmanuel—God with us* aspect of their faith captivated my heart. Looking back over my life, I only knew the term Emmanuel as associated with Christmas. The promise of the coming Messiah, the *Emmanuel—God with us* found in Isaiah 7:14, is also recorded in Matthew 1:23. There the angel tells Joseph in a dream that he should marry Mary. These verses were always front and center in the church as we approached, and then celebrated, the birth of the Christ child. The concept lingered, perhaps a week or two longer, and then, almost unobtrusively, we packed it away with the nativity scene and the rest of the tree ornaments.

Each year, as we celebrate Christmas, we rejoice in *Emmanuel—God with us*. Yet for most of the year—therefore most of our lives—we live as if He is not with us, except when we find him in those carved-out scheduled "quiet times." But we do not need to merely settle for an hour in the morning in the hope of encountering the living Christ.

If we truly believe God's Word, that He is *Emmanuel—God with us*, then we should expect to experience Him in our regular daily lives.

Celtic Christianity has taught me that living an *Emmanuel—God with us* life will transform your world. My life has been richer and my spiritual walk deeper since I began to embrace God as Emmanuel.

No longer do I carefully pack Him away each year after the Christmas celebration has passed. No longer do I only hope to experience Him when reading my Bible or praying. Instead, I expect to meet Him in the midst of my ordinary day, in every moment and in every way. I look for Him and find Him in the mundane as well as in ministry. Now I walk every day in the assurance that He is with me and that He will never leave me nor forsake me.

Ponder:

Describe your experience with Emmanuel. Do you expect to find Him in the midst of your ordinary day? What encounters with the living God have blessed your life?

Dwell:

Sit with the truth that the God of all creation, the Holy One of Israel, the King of Kings and Lord of Lords, delights to walk alongside you every minute of every day. Revel in the knowledge that our great warrior King is your protector and your faithful friend.

Action:

Ask God to open the eyes of your heart that you may see Him at work in your daily life. Journaling your encounters with Him will increase your ability to experience a richer and deeper walk with your God.

My flesh and my heart may fail,
but God is the strength of my heart and my portion forever.

PSALM 73:26

Psalm 73:26, the most underlined and dated scripture in my Bible, speaks to me more than mere words. It has provided a lifeline on more occasions than I have even recorded. One of these took place the year my first husband left our family. Along with my children I struggled with this new chapter in our lives.

For financial reasons we had to move out of our home. God led us to an apartment not far from our familiar neighborhood. This meant that the children could continue to attend the same schools. Later that year, I enrolled at Glasgow University. I also had a part-time placement requirement to fulfill in a Church of Scotland congregation.

In this full life, hope and strength disappeared. My greatest concern was for my children. They appeared to do well, but their pain and sadness became evident to their mother's heart. Each of them needed extra love and encouragement. When they went to school or out to play, I often wept till I ran out of tears. I called out to God to help me, and He responded to my cry. I sensed Him say to me, "These children are your first priority. Give them all the time they need. Make them know that you will never go away without them."

In the very depth of my being, these words came to me as a commandment. I made a promise that day to God and myself: I would seek to fulfill His words. I knew this would help my kids rebuild a sense of security. I also knew I had a lot on my plate, including my own mountain of homework. What God asked of me would leave little time to attend to it. My heart and mind became set. I would need to trust in my heavenly Father. I could do no other.

My daughter Fiona loved to play board games. Every night after the children had finished their homework, we would have family time. We played the board game of choice, discussed Star Trek and the upcoming convention, and chatted about old and new worship songs. We prayed at bedtime. By 10:00 p.m. silence reigned. Now, I could begin to address the reading and writing that were required for my classes.

I would study and write from 10:00 p.m. till 2:00 a.m. If I couldn't cover all the work in that time, it didn't get done. It became clear I didn't have time to cover every chapter of the required books. All too often I had to settle for only reading the introduction and the conclusion. I was concerned I would fail all of my classes. I hadn't anticipated the miraculous taking place. At least, it appeared miraculous to me. Every paper I submitted and every exam I wrote came back with a very good grade. I have no idea what the professors read. I often think they did not see the words I had written, but an improved version that God wrote.

As I lived faithfully in what God asked of me, He responded faithfully to me. My heart and my strength almost disappeared, but God became my strength and my portion forever. He still is.

Ponder:

God longs to give you strength in whatever situation weighs on your heart.

Dwell:

Soak in the truth that God promises to trade your weariness and weakness for His presence and His power.

Action:

1. Make a list of things, people, or situations that trouble you. Take time now to talk to God about these concerns. He will rejoice that you did.

2. Write, "God is the strength of my heart and my portion forever" on a card or piece of paper and place it in your wallet or purse, or on your mirror, counter, desk, or dashboard—somewhere prominent. When something begins to distress you, read these words and allow their truth to fill you with the knowledge that you are not alone. He is with you, and He will carry you through.

And my God will meet all your needs
according to his glorious riches in Christ Jesus.

PHILIPPIANS 4:19

At the age of five, I could not wait for Christmas. "What would you like Santa to bring you?" The answer was simple, "A bride doll." No matter how often and no matter who did the asking the answer remained the same, "A bride doll." I had no desire for anything else.

My mother, standing by my side and listening to my answer, would smile. Her smile did not betray for one second the sadness and anxiety she felt deep within her heart. Watching the beaming face of her youngest child as she told one and all that this Christmas she would be getting a bride doll became hard to bear. How could she make this happen?

With little money, and with four other children who also deserved a happy Christmas, an expensive bride doll was out of the question. The hope and child-like faith she saw in her daughter's eyes cut her to the bone. The nearer it came to Christmas, the heavier her heart felt. She started rehearsing what she would say to soften the blow of disappointment when no doll appeared among the presents. Faith had always played a key role in her life, but a bride doll somehow seemed impossible.

Two days before Christmas the local Brethren church held a Christmas party for the neighborhood children. They provided fun, food, singing, games, and, of course, a visit from Santa. Every child received a present. I carried mine home with great care. I placed it under the small tree ready to be opened on Christmas morning.

Christmas morning came, and we opened our gifts. I only have memory of one: the one from Santa—the one that he had given to me at the church party. When I opened it, my eyes lit up, my heart sang, and I was the happiest girl in the world. I held in my hands the most beautiful bride doll ever. Six inches tall, with blue eyes, and blond hair. She wore a white brocade dress and a net veil. A painted band with a sparkle in the middle adorned the ring finger of her left hand.

I never noticed the tears of thanksgiving trickling down my mother's face. Years later as an adult, I learned her side of the story. That Christmas, my mother knew for sure that God had met her needs according to His riches in Christ Jesus.

God has no favorites. His promises belong to all His children. He is Jehovah Jireh, our Provider.

Ponder:

Do you have a favorite story of God's provision in your life? Take a few minutes to recall the details.

Dwell:

Allow the memory to go deep into your heart. Linger there, remembering His goodness to you.

Action:

Write a short prayer of thanksgiving.

Be exalted, O God, above the heavens,
and let your glory be over all the earth.

PSALM 108:5

These words appear three times in the Psalms: twice, in Psalm 57, and once in Psalm 108. Both of these psalms combine lament and praise. In Psalm 57, praise follows lament, and in Psalm 108, lament follows praise. The laments differ, but the praise in both psalms remains the same:

My heart is steadfast, O God; I will sing and make music with all my soul. Awake, harp and lyre! I will awaken the dawn. I will praise you, O Lord, among the nations; I will sing of you among the peoples. For great is your love, higher than the heavens; your faithfulness reaches to the skies. Be exalted, O God, above the heavens, and let your glory be over all the earth.

These psalms reflect the fact that sometimes we lay all our worry and concerns before God and, having done so, we feel able to praise Him. Other times, we find ourselves praising Him, and out of our praise we confidently tell Him what is weighing heavily on our hearts. Most importantly He helps us get to the place where our hearts become steadfast—set, ready, and able to remember Him and His great care for us.

The Celtic faith found God in the midst of creation, as the psalmist often did. Some accused Celtic Christians of creationism—worshipping creation. This was a false perception. They directed their worship at the One who created the heavens and earth and everything in them. For them, God's glory extended over and in all the earth. They prayed to this end, they wrote poetry to this end, and they lived to this end. "God of the Moon," one of their poems reflects this:

God of the moon, God of the sun,
God of the globe, God of the stars,
God of the waters, the land, and the skies,
Who ordained to us the King of promise.

It was Mary fair, who went upon her knee,
It was the King of life that went upon her lap.
Darkness and tears were set behind,
And the star of guidance went up early.

Illumed the land, illumed the world,
Illumed doldrum and current.
Grief was laid and joy was raised,
Music was set up with harp and pedal-harp.[i]

May we like the psalmist and the Celts find our Creator God to be faithful.

Ponder:

The lyrics of the traditional children's hymn, "God, Who Made the Earth," always comforted me as a young girl. May their truth remind you of God's creative love.

God, who made the earth,
The air, the sky, the sea,
Who gave the light its birth,
He cares for me.

God, who made the grass,
The flow'r, the fruit, the tree,
The day and night to pass,
He cares for me.

What comfort does this give you, today?

Dwell:

God, who made the sun,
The moon, the stars, is He,
Who, when life's clouds come on,
He cares for me.

God, who made all things,
On earth, in air, in sea,
Who if I lean on Him,
Will care for me.[ii]

Action:

During this Advent season, we often find ourselves unable to join in with the "ho, ho, ho," or the jingle-bell music. Write a prayer of lament to God, and then praise Him for who He is and who you are to Him.

Praise be to the God and Father of our Lord Jesus Christ,
the Father of compassion and the God of all comfort.
2 Corinthians 1:3

The image of God as Father can have negative connotations for many Christians. If a child experienced their earthly father as unpleasant, nonexistent, or abusive, it makes relating to God as our heavenly Father very difficult. Personally, I fall into the category of nonexistent. More accurately the term would be absent. My father did not come to the hospital to see my mother at my birth, and he remained more or less absent from that point on. I only have two vague memories of him.

I have to admit I never found relating to God as a parent figure very problematic. I attribute this to the fact that my mum always seemed to cover all the bases for both parents. I did have some issues with abandonment. Happily I received inner healing prayer for these, and the issues eventually subsided. Having said that, I have spent countless hours with enough wounded souls to know not everyone's journey has resolved so easily.

Over the centuries many misconceptions about God and His true nature have appeared. Legalistic religious leaders and angry earthly fathers, who have by their lifestyles distorted His true image, have misrepresented Him to us. When our earthly fathers have fallen short of how they should have treated us, we often transfer these deficiencies onto God, our heavenly Father. We must separate truth from lies when this happens. The best way to do this is to turn to Scripture. As we do this, we see that God is not distant and angry as many of the Renaissance paintings portrayed Him. Rather He is loving, gentle, and kind.

Since God created us for love, we are born with a great expectation to be loved and accepted. God's desire was to enter into a personal relationship with all His children. The closest and most tender relationship the Bible portrays is that of "Father." This was Christ's most common designation for the One to whom He prayed and of whom He taught.

The *Father's Love Letter*, from Father Heart Communications, played a significant role in the healing of my abandonment issues. The words, taken from Scripture, provided the truth I needed. I continue to find a new level of peace each time I read the words or listen to them via the website: www.fathersLoveLetter.com.

The concept is a letter from God to all of humanity based on Scripture. This letter overflows with words of hope, grace, peace, and assurance. It reminds us that we are made in God's image and that before we were even born He knew us. "You were not a mistake," is one of the phrases that touched my heart at a very deep level. I desired to spend more time in God's presence when I learned that He desired to lavish His love on me simply because I am his child and He is my Father. Knowing that He is close to me when I am brokenhearted fills me with peace.

God is "head over heels in love" with us, and He longs to be in relationship with you and with me. He is the ultimate and only perfect Father, and He cares more deeply about us than we could ever hope or imagine.

Ponder:

God does not keep a ledger in heaven so that He will not over-bless us. We can never use up our quota of our heavenly Father's compassion, mercy, and love. And we can never overestimate His tenderness toward His own, which includes you and me!

Dwell:

However intimate, rich, and warmhearted His love, God remains God, majestic, all-powerful, righteous, and holy. And One certainly worthy of our honor and praise.

Action:

Write a prayer or a poem that acknowledges God your heavenly Father as indeed the Father of compassion and the God of all comfort. In this prayer ask Him to protect you from the evil one who seeks to keep us from seeing and knowing the true character of our Abba Father, Daddy.

Week Two
Light the **HOLY SPIRIT** Candle

The angel answered,
The **Holy Spirit** will come upon
you,
and the power of the Most High
will overshadow you.
So the holy one to be born will
be called the Son of God.
Luke 1:35

Now the earth was formless and empty,
darkness was over the surface of the deep,
and the Spirit of God was hovering over the waters.

GENESIS 1:2

We tend to picture the Holy Spirit as a New Testament addition to the faith. Pentecost provides the big "ta-da" moment when the Holy Spirit becomes part of the divine leadership team. This is false.

Genesis 1:1: "In the beginning God created the heavens and the earth," but God the Father wasn't alone. The Holy Spirit was also present. Genesis 1:2 makes that clear. More than this, Jesus was there with them. John 1:1-3 explains, "In the beginning was the Word, and the Word was with God, and the Word was God. He was with God in the beginning. Through Him all things were made; without him nothing was made that has been made."

All three: Father, Son, and Holy Spirit presided when the earth was formless and darkness was over the surface of the deep. The work of three Persons brought about Creation: Unified in design and unified in decisions. In the beginning, we see the work of divine hearts and minds in perfect harmony; we sense agreement, one with the other and we experience a unity forged from an unmatched love.

Unity forms one of the greatest lessons that creation teaches us. Unity lies at the heart of the Gospel message. The psalmist also speaks this message: "How good and pleasant it is when God's people live together in unity" (Psalm 133:1). Fundamental to unity is love. The apostle John makes it clear that, although this headlines Jesus' teaching, it began long before His earthly ministry. "This is the message you heard from the beginning: We should love one another" (1 John 3:11).

Shortly before Jesus died, He prayed with His disciples. He prayed for Himself, for the disciples, and then for all believers. In His prayer for the believers—you and me—He said, "I have given them the glory that you gave me, that they may be one as we are one—I in them and you in me—so that they may be brought to complete unity. Then the world will know that you sent me and have loved them even as you have loved me" (John 17:22–23).

When Jesus told the disciples that He would no longer remain with them, He promised them another "Paraclete"—another Counselor—the Spirit of truth, in His place. He specified the role of the Holy Spirit. "All this I have spoken while still with you. But the Counselor, the Holy Spirit, whom the Father will send in my name, will teach you all things and will remind you of everything I have said to you" (John 14:25–26).

Today, the Holy Spirit, who was present at creation, unified with the Father and the Son, reminds us of the importance and basis of unity in the body of Christ. "A new command I give you: Love one another. As I have loved you, so you must love one another. By this everyone will know that you are my disciples, if you love one another" (John 13:34–35).

Ponder:

Make every effort to keep the unity of the Spirit through the bond of peace (Ephesians 4:3).

Dwell:

Holy Spirit, Truth divine,
Dawn upon this soul of mine;
Word of God, and inward Light,
Wake my spirit, clear my sight.

Holy Spirit, Peace Divine,
Still this restless heart of mine;
Speak to calm this tossing sea,
Stayed in Thy tranquility.[iii]

Action:

What areas of your life does disunity cloud? List three of them:

1.

2.

3.

Invite the Holy Spirit to help you find the path to unity for each situation.

*And I have filled him with the Spirit of God,
with wisdom and understanding, with knowledge and with in all kinds of
skills.*

EXODUS 31:3

God filled Bezalel with His Spirit. The first five verses of Exodus 31 explain: "Then the LORD said to Moses, 'See, I have chosen Bezalel son of Uri, the son of Hur, of the tribe of Judah, and I have filled him with the Spirit of God, with wisdom, with understanding, with knowledge and with all kinds of skills—to make artistic designs for work in gold, silver and bronze, to cut and set stones, to work in wood, and to engage in all kinds of crafts.' "

In Exodus 24 we learn that the people of God accepted His covenant and met with Him on Mount Sinai. In order to maintain His presence, God mandated the building of a tabernacle where He would dwell and His presence would continue with His people. In chapter 28, God filled the embroiderers with His spirit of wisdom, and in Chapter 31, He chose and filled Bezalel with His Spirit.

In this passage, Bezalel is revealed as the first person to receive the Spirit of God, the Holy Spirit. The Holy Spirit equipped Bezalel with skill and ability; to give him knowledge in all kinds of skills; to make artistic designs; to cut and set stones; to engage in all kinds of craftsmanship. These gifts of the Spirit rarely receive mention. Instead, we focus on the New Testament accounts of the Holy Spirit. By doing so we miss out on the creative aspect of the Holy Spirit's work.

Although this may come as news to many of us, it formed a way of life and faith for the early Celtic Christians. These gifts of skill, ability, and creative knowledge, given by the Spirit of God to Bezalel, became second nature to them. The *Book of Kells*, the *Lindisfarne Gospels*, and other documents reveal some of the most prominent demonstrations of these gifts.

The *Book of Kells* is breathtaking. It contains a rich, illuminated manuscript of the four gospels. You can see it on display in Dublin's Trinity College Library. Originating as early as St. Columba, in the sixth century, the ornamentation and illustrations exhibit exquisite beauty. I felt transported back in time when I stood there, gazing upon it. Awe and wonder permeated my being. These ancient brothers and sisters who painstakingly used the gifts of the Spirit continued to bless me that day.

The Spirit inspired other examples of Celtic art. High crosses, found north of Dublin at Monasterboice, have majestic carvings of many biblical stories. The Holy Spirit is a creative Spirit, and the Celts bear testimony to this truth.

Ponder:

The Holy Spirit fills us with many different gifts. "Now to each one the manifestation of the Spirit is given for the common good. To one there is given through the Spirit the message of wisdom, to another the message of knowledge by means of the same Spirit, to another faith by the same Spirit, to another gifts of healing by that one Spirit, to another miraculous powers, to another prophecy, to another distinguishing between spirits, to another speaking in different kinds of tongues, and to still another the interpretation of tongues. All these are the work of one and the same Spirit, and he distributes them to each one, just as he determines" (1 Corinthians 12:7–11).

Dwell:

Some claim the *Book of Kells* as the most beautiful book in the world. Its colorful, artistic mastery depicts the life and ministry of Christ. Miniscule human and animal figures appear within the capital letters that begin each major segment. These figures also occur in the margins and in other unexpected places.

Before the invention of printing, the hands of scribes created these illuminated Gospels and other holy manuscripts. It took years for the creation of each one. The skill and patience needed came from the Holy Spirit. Throughout the centuries, this work has blessed and transformed countless lives.

Action:

Imagine these saints painstakingly laboring for many years on a manuscript. No ready-made paint box, colored pencils, or art supplies. They created an act of love, inspired by the Holy Spirit and carefully carried out.

Write or say a prayer of thanksgiving for all those who dedicated their lives to ensure that all generations would know the Gospel of Jesus Christ.

Day 3 Holy Spirit

November 21

But the Counselor, the Holy Spirit, whom the Father will send in my name, will teach you all things and will remind you of everything I have said to you.

JOHN 14:26

I love the Holy Spirit. As each week, month, and year passes, my love for Him grows. Yet, in the churches I attended while growing up, I only remember strong teaching on the Father and the Son. My memories of those years create a picture of the Holy Spirit in the role of an understudy.

In my thirties, a friend invited me to attend a Women's Aglow meeting. I went along and found these people in touch with the Holy Spirit. As a Presbyterian, the experience overwhelmed me. However, I started attending regularly because I loved their passion for Christ and His Word. Anita, the president, was a gentle and loving lady. Aware that I did not fully buy into their enthusiasm for the Holy Spirit, she called me. She read several Scriptures to me in the hope that I would see the importance the Spirit.

As she was speaking, I am embarrassed to admit, I was rolling my eyes. Although I never said so out loud, in my head I thought, *I don't care if it's in the Bible, if it's not taught in my church I am not interested.* My theology was poor. Several years went by before I began to bring down the barriers I had erected against knowing the Holy Spirit.

When I did, I found that He fulfilled all that the Word says He is: Counselor, Comforter, Companion, Speaker of Truth, Reminder of all Christ has said, Source of Power, Third and Equal Person of the Trinity.

I suspect that, the evil one has used speaking in tongues and the prophetic aspect of the Holy Spirit, which some branches of the church have elevated, to hold the mainline churches in ransom. Focus on the Spirit's manifestations has buried His role and person under the soil of fear, resulting in His power going MIA, missing in action.

Toward the end of writing my doctoral thesis, I realized that I had omitted a section on the Holy Spirit. The work focused on prayer, with an emphasis on healing and inner healing prayer. This topic remained incomplete without addressing the role of the Spirit. With time growing short I made the decision to research only what the Bible says about the third person of the Trinity. God's Word revealed to me the role and person of His Holy Spirit, and I entered into an ever-deepening relationship that has enriched my life and spiritual journey.

Throughout Scripture God sends His Holy Spirit on many different people, including His Son. He did so because He knew that each one needed the power, guidance, and support that could only come through the role and person of the Spirit. God waited patiently for me to embrace His Spirit. I am grateful He did.

Daily, I am aware of how much I need the Holy Spirit to teach me all things and to remind me of everything my Savior has said.

Ponder:

What has been your experience of the Holy Spirit? Intimate relationship? Vague notion of who He is? Never given it much thought?

Dwell:

"And I will ask the Father, and he will give you another counselor to help you and be with you forever—the Spirit of truth. The world cannot accept him, because it neither sees him nor knows him. But you know him, for he lives with you and will be in you" (John 14:16–17).

Action:

Ask the Father to give you a deeper revelation of the role and person of the Holy Spirit. Record what He shows you.

*Jesus, full of the Holy Spirit, returned from the Jordan
and was led by the Spirit in the desert.*

LUKE 4:1

Chapter 3, verses 21-22 of Luke's Gospel tell us, "When all the people were being baptized, Jesus was baptized too. And as he was praying, heaven was opened and the Holy Spirit descended on him in bodily form like a dove. And a voice came from heaven: 'You are my Son, whom I love; with you I am well pleased.' " The only information that separates these words from our Scripture for today is a genealogy, tracing Jesus back to God.

The Holy Spirit, who came on Jesus at His baptism and filled Him, now leads Him into the desert. This trip was not a pleasure trip. It would become a test. For forty days the devil tempted Jesus. During this time Jesus did not eat any food. The forty-day period concluded with the three tests recorded in Luke 4:4-12 and Matthew 4:1-13.

Test 1

The devil said to him, "If you are the Son of God, tell this stone to become bread."

Jesus answered, "It is written: 'Man does not live on bread alone' " (Luke 4:3-4).

The Score: Jesus 1 The devil 0

Test 2

The devil led him up to a high place and showed him in an instant all the kingdoms of the world. And he said to him, "I will give you all their authority and splendor, for it has been given to me, and I can give it to anyone I want to. So if you worship me, it will all be yours."

Jesus answered, "It is written: 'Worship the Lord your God and serve him only' " (Luke 4:5-8).

The New Score: Jesus 2 The devil 0

Test 3

The devil led him to Jerusalem and had him stand on the highest point of the temple. "If you are the Son of God," he said, "throw yourself down from here. For it is written, 'He will command his angels concerning you to guard you carefully; they will lift you up in their hands, so that you will not strike your foot against a stone.' "

Jesus answered, "It says: 'Do not put the Lord your God to the test' " (Luke 4:9-12).

Final Score: Jesus 3 The devil 0

The devil left, and Jesus returned to Galilee in the *power of the Holy Spirit*. News about him spread through the whole countryside (italics added).

The Spirit *led* Jesus into the desert. The devil *led* him to a high place and then to Jerusalem. Jesus' victory over the wiles of the devil did not come from His divine power. When the Word became flesh, He set His divinity aside and lived out of His humanity. How in His human strength, did He resist these temptations? The power of the Holy Spirit accomplished this.

Jesus entered the desert filled with the Holy Spirit and it was through this power that He defeated the evil set before Him. God offers that same Spirit, that same power, to each one of Christ's followers.

Ponder:

For what areas of temptation in your life do you need to draw on the Holy Spirit's power and strength?

Dwell:

"But you will receive power when the Holy Spirit comes on you; and you will be my witnesses in Jerusalem, and in all Judea and Samaria, and to the ends of the earth" (Acts 1:8).

Action:

Invite the Holy Spirit to fill you afresh with His power. Thank the Father for sending Him to you. Praise Jesus for not leaving us to walk through our earthly life without divine help.

May the grace of the Lord Jesus Christ, and the love of God,
and the fellowship of the Holy Spirit be with you all.

2 CORINTHIANS 13:14

The Celtic Christians accepted God—Father, Son, and Holy Spirit—unreservedly. They did not need to understand this concept at some deep or intellectual level. God in three persons had become a truth to believe and a threefold relationship to embrace. This fact emerges in a great number of their prayers. To underscore their comfort with the three-in-one Godhead, they used various analogies from nature and daily life.

An old traditional poem from Ireland reflects this:

Three folds of the cloth, yet only one napkin is there,
Three joints in the finger, but still only one finger fair,
Three leaves of the shamrock, yet no more than one shamrock to wear,
Frost, snowflakes and ice, all in water their origins share
Three Persons in God; to one God alone we make prayer.

Carmina Gadelica and the *Religious Songs of Connacht* bear witness of the Trinity's great importance to our brothers and sisters of long ago. The daily labor songs and the seasonal work songs demonstrated the centrality of God—Father, Son, and Holy Spirit. Their day began with three handfuls of water splashed on their faces in the name of the three members of the Trinity. In doing this, they took the presence of the Trinity with them.

I now incorporate this into my daily life. First thing in the morning, as I wash my face, I welcome the Trinity into my day. I splash the water on my face in the evening as I prepare for bed, giving the Three in One praise for another day.

There are many prayers that reflect how deeply the Celtic Christians believed in and relied on all three persons of the Trinity. St. Patrick's Breastplate is probably the most famous. The last stanza says this:

> I bind unto myself the name,
> The strong name of the Trinity,
> By invocation of the same,
> The Three in One and One in Three,
> Of whom all nature has creation;
> Eternal Father, Spirit, Word,
> Praise to the Lord of my salvation,
> Salvation is of Christ the Lord.

May we, like the ancient Celts, know and experience the grace of the Lord Jesus Christ, the love of God, and the fellowship of the Holy Spirit, today and always.

Ponder:

Traditionally, many prayers end with the threefold benediction: In the name of the Father and the Son and Holy Spirit. How do you feel about praying directly to each person of the Trinity?

Dwell:

"I keep asking that the God of our Lord Jesus Christ, the glorious Father, may give you the Spirit of wisdom and revelation, so that you may know him better" (Ephesians 1:17).

Action:

Calvin Miller, writing in *The Path of Celtic Prayer*, encourages his readers to practice writing a Trinity prayer. He gives the following prayer as an example for evening use:

God of all that is and was and shall be,
For this day and its fullness, I give you thanks;
Thank you, Father, for the Earth and for all its endless beauty.
Thank you especially for:

Thank you, Son, for, your example of obedience
To your Father which taught me faithfulness this day
As I endeavored to:

Thank you, Spirit, for your infilling of my life,
I especially thank you for your presence today
As you walked with me through:

In the same way, the Spirit helps us in our weakness.
We do not know what we ought to pray for,
but the Spirit himself intercedes for us
through wordless groans.

ROMANS 8:26

Life as parents of young children can exhaust our strength. I have three kids, all grown now, but I remember those early years so well. Sleepless nights and busy days often formed the norm for my schedule as a stay-at-home mom, an elder in our church, the editor of the church magazine, and neighborhood salesperson for Avon.

At the birth of my daughter Fiona, my oldest son Fraser was five and my youngest son Greig was thirteen months. Our morning routine consisted of breakfast for everyone. Then Fraser prepared for school. Most Scottish schools have a set uniform that the pupils are required to wear. Moms, this removes any discussions, arguments, or hissy fits about what your children might want to choose.

We could easily walk to the school from our house. With my husband off to work, I would put the baby in the "high" pram and put Greig, in the seat that clipped over the pram body. Fraser walked at my side. I used a brown Silver Cross classic carriage pram. British mothers often prefer this style of pram for new babies. With Fraser safely in school, I would walk back home and begin the routine of the day: Put the kids down for a nap and then do washing, ironing, cleaning, etc.

Fiona was probably four months old the day I changed my routine. I became so tired that I could hardly function. So, with my kids asleep, I decided that I would take a nap at the same time. I put Greig in his crib and, as usual, let Fiona sleep in her pram. I fell gratefully into bed and went to sleep before my head hit the pillow. I have no idea how long I slept before I heard someone calling my name. "Jean. Jean." I slowly began to wake. I thought, *it must be my imagination. I am the only adult in the house. Who could be calling my name?* I started to fall back to sleep. "Jean. Jean." The voice came again.

I grew confused, in that "not awake and not fully asleep" place. It made no sense to me. How could someone be calling my name? The voice persisted, but this time with a greater sense of urgency. "JEAN. JEAN." The urgency forced me fully awake. I got up and ran into Greig's room, where I found him safe and still asleep. Then I ran downstairs to the living room where I had left Fiona. Somehow she had dislodged the pram quilt that I had tucked in around her. It now covered her face. Her muffled, frantic cries registered her fight against suffocation. I quickly pulled the baby quilt off, lifted her into my arms, and gratefully held her until she recovered.

The voice I heard was neither male nor female, but I know it was real. It may have been the voice of an angel or even the voice of God, Himself. I have always believed that God's Holy Spirit saw what happened and interceded before the Father's throne on our behalf. I did not know I needed to pray. Happily, the Holy Spirit did, and God answered in the most amazing way.

Ponder:

The Spirit helps us in our weakness. We do not know what we ought to pray, but the Spirit Himself intercedes for us with groans that words cannot express. This takes on many different forms. What has this looked like in your life?

Dwell:

God has set a safeguard in place for us. When we don't know what to pray, or that we even need to pray, the Holy Spirit intercedes on our behalf. More than this, Jesus himself also prays on our behalf. "My prayer is not that you take them out of the world but that you protect them from the evil one" (John 17:15).

Action:

Jesus also said, "My prayer is not for them alone. I pray also for those who will believe in me through their message" (John 17:20). What is the message you will be sharing this Advent?

Write down three things that would be at the heart of your message. Then ask Jesus to pray to the Father that, in this season, people in your sphere of influence will come to believe in Him.

1.

2.

3.

Day 7 Holy Spirit November 25

Do not cast me from your presence
or take your Holy Spirit from me.

PSALM 51:11

David pleads with God for spiritual restoration. He appeals to the "unfailing love" (*hesed*) of God as the basis of hope for forgiveness. Although David has failed through sin, Yahweh does not fail. He continues in His commitment to David and to all sinful human beings who acknowledge their sin and rely on His merciful forgiveness and love.

When we trace the Holy Spirit/God's Spirit throughout the Bible we find a clear progression of the endowment of the Spirit by God, manifested in three stages:

Stage 1—Temporary and Limited Endowment

Stage 2—Full, Personal, and Permanent Endowment on Jesus

Stage 3—Full, Personal, and Permanent Endowment on the Church

Stage 1—Temporary and Limited Endowment

In the Old Testament, the Spirit made God's will and wisdom known to His people. This often came through the phenomenon of "prophecy," when the Spirit, in a dream, vision, or word granted a message of the Lord. However, this kind of endowment was temporary. For example, in 1 Samuel 10:10, Saul receives the Spirit. In 16:14 we read how God took His Spirit from Saul. This sets the scene for a repentant David to pray, "Do not . . . take your Holy Spirit from me" (Psalm 51:11). In the Old

Testament, when God chose to give His Spirit, it did not remain permanent. Instead, He gave it to *selective people, for specific purposes, at certain times* in history.

Stage 2—Full and Permanent Endowment on Jesus

In Isaiah 61:1–2 we read that the Spirit would come upon the Messiah. As the promised Messiah, conceived by the Holy Spirit, Jesus' life and ministry manifested the work of the Spirit. Luke highlights that, when Jesus entered the synagogue at Nazareth on the Sabbath and read from the prophet Isaiah, He claimed to fulfill the prophecy of this passage. "The Spirit of the Lord is on me, because he has appointed me to preach good news to the poor. He has sent me to proclaim freedom for the prisoners and recovery of sight for the blind, to release the oppressed, to proclaim the year of the Lord's favor . . . Today this scripture is fulfilled in your hearing" (Luke 4:18, 19, 21).

The Gospels acknowledge the role of the Spirit in Jesus' life. Yet this endowment of the Spirit differed from the endowment we read about in the Hebrew Scriptures. Jesus received a full, personal, and permanent endowment of the Spirit.

Stage 3—Full, Personal, and Permanent Endowment on the Church

Christ promised His disciples this same power, this same permanence, and this same measure. Scripture bears witness to the fact that at Pentecost the gift of the Holy Spirit would become permanent and personal. In John 14:16–17 Jesus tells His disciples that, "I will ask the Father, and he will give you another Counselor to help you and be with you *forever*—the Spirit of truth" (emphasis added). Acts tells us, "They saw what seemed to be tongues of fire that separated and came to rest on *each of them. All of them* were filled with the Holy Spirit . . ." (2:3–4, emphasis added).

This *third stage* remains one of the most important keys for the success of the church and for our personal walk with God. Here we see the permanent and personal endowment of the Spirit given to individual believers in the same measure Christ received it. Unlike David, we need not fear that the Holy Spirit will be taken from us. God has given Him to us forever. What a wonderful gift!

Ponder:

During Jesus' ministry, there is no reference to the Holy Spirit coming upon anyone except Jesus. There is reference in the Gospels to the Spirit coming upon certain people before Jesus began his ministry, e.g., Mary, Zachariah, Elizabeth, John the Baptist, and Simeon. Like the endowment of the Spirit on the Old Testament characters, these anointed events remained temporary.

Dwell:

By the complete, personal, limitless, infilling of the Holy Spirit, Jesus fulfilled His ministry and communicated with His Father.

Jesus overcame evil in the desert through the power and person of the Holy Spirit.

He carried out His ministry of healing through the power and person of the Holy Spirit.

Jesus spent time in intimate prayer with the Father, spoke to Him, and heard His voice through the power and person of the Holy Spirit.

In the Garden of Gethsemane, He said "Your will be done not mine," through the power and person of the Holy Spirit.

Jesus walked up that hill to Calvary's cross through the power and person of the Holy Spirit.

Action:

Praise God that He has given you a *Full, Personal, and Permanent Endowment of His Holy Spirit*. List three areas of your life that will benefit from living in this truth.

1.

2.

3.

Week Three
Light the **HOPE** Candle

We wait in
hope
for the Lord;
he is our help and our shield.
Psalm 33:20

But as for me, I watch in hope for the LORD, I wait for God my Savior; my God will hear me.

MICAH 7:7

St. Cuthbert lived in the seventh century. As a Celtic monk who followed in the footsteps of St. Aiden, he sought to bring the light and love of Christ to all people. He ministered in southern Scotland and also in Northumbria, in the northeastern part of England. Although he held positions of authority and influence in the monastery, the ordinary people in the surrounding districts became his passion. He worked to engage and encourage them with the hope and belief that they would come to love God and His ways. Cuthbert often left the monastery on foot and preached the truth of the Gospel in neighboring towns.

The effect of Cuthbert's life in Christ and his hope in God appears in countless stories. For example, according to one story, as recorded in Bede's *"The Life of Cuthbert,"* Cuthbert and two brothers travelled to the land of Niduari, to a tribe of Picts.

They landed safely, but a storm arose and cut them off from all help. Cuthbert, in an effort to give his companions hope, stated:

"Why do we remain listless and unresourceful?" he asked. "We ought to be thinking over every possible way of saving ourselves. The land is bleak with snow, clouds lour in the sky, there is a gale raging and the sea is a fury of waves, we are dying of hunger and there is no chance of human aid. Then let us storm Heaven with our prayers, asking that the same Lord who parted the Red Sea and fed His people in the desert take pity on us in our peril."[iv]

God heard their prayers, took pity on them, and met their needs.

Cuthbert's greatest ministry took place on Lindisfarne, also known as the Holy Isle. Twice a day it becomes an island when the tide comes in. When I visited there, I experienced the rich rhythm this island provides. A gentle peace descends, and the inability to go anywhere else becomes a God-given gift. Cuthbert embraced this gift but longed for an even deeper solitude. He found this solitude on a smaller island close to Lindisfarne. This little island on the Inner Farne now bears his name.

Cuthbert desired a place where he could enter into intimate prayer with God: speaking and listening. This island met his needs. It had no water, food, or trees. Here in this place, Cuthbert communed with God. Prayer became the food of life for him.

My "must do" list includes a visit to St. Cuthbert's Island. I desire to spend time there in prayer. I long to drink from the well of God's presence that flooded Cuthbert's soul. I crave the depth of hope this ancient Celt displayed.

Ponder:

"When you say a situation or a person is hopeless, you're slamming the door in the face of God." Charles L. Allen

Dwell:

"One thing I ask from the LORD, this only do I seek: that I may dwell in the house of the LORD all the days of my life, to gaze upon the beauty of the Lord and to seek him in his temple. For in the day of trouble he will keep me safe in his dwelling; he will hide me in the shelter of his sacred tent and set me high upon a rock" (Psalm 27:4–5).

Action:

Throughout this Advent week of Hope, take time to give Jesus your fears and tell Him about all that is in your longing heart. You may wish to write out your thoughts below as a prayer.

And again, Isaiah says, "The Root of Jesse will spring up, one who will arise to rule over the nations; in him the Gentiles will hope."

ROMANS 15:12

Paul, writing here to the church in Rome, quotes the prophet Isaiah. Paul focuses on unity as one of his central themes. Disagreement reigns in the lives of Christ's followers. The issue stems from the division between Jewish believers and their Gentile counterparts.

In verses 7 through 12, these Christians are urged by Paul to "accept one another, then, just as Christ accepted you, in order to bring praise to God. For I tell you that Christ has become a servant of the Jews on behalf of God's truth, so that the promises made to the patriarchs might be confirmed and, moreover, that the Gentiles might glorify God for his mercy."

God's plan for salvation did not remain limited to Israel and the Jewish people. His desire was for all to come to a saving knowledge of Him through His Son Jesus Christ. What a glorious gift.

To us, the Gentiles, these words of Scripture bring encouragement and hope. Paul, quoting Isaiah 11:10, reminds us that God had a plan in place even before Christ became flesh and dwelt among us. That plan was to bring hope out of despair and life out of death.

This root of Jesse is the foundation of the words in Isaiah 11:1: "A shoot will come up from the stump of Jesse; from his roots a Branch will bear fruit." Jesse fathered King David and so this "Branch," the Messiah, would indeed come from the line of David.

The genealogy of Christ occurs in both Matthew's and Luke's gospels. Luke's account traces Jesus back to God, while Matthew traces Jesus' lineage back to Abraham.

Matthew's account has captured the hearts and minds of artists for centuries. Their work has focused on the "Jesse" aspect of the Isaiah text. They have beautifully depicted the tree of Jesse, Christ's family tree, in stained glass, illuminated manuscripts, paintings, and much more. Many of these artists have incorporated a reclining image of Jesse with a tree coming out of his middle.

The earliest stained glass example of the Jesse Tree appears in northern France in Chartres Cathedral. This magnificent, twelfth-century window is breathtaking. It depicts the royal genealogy on the central panel and the images of fourteen prophets, seven on each of the side panels.

In recent years, Jesse trees have become another way to celebrate the hope we have in Advent. We can use a single branch, or a small tree, or even a simple paper drawing and then add Scriptures or symbols representing the journey from creation to Christ. Another type of Jesse tree traces the story from Jesse to Jesus. A Jesse tree can serve as a great visual lesson to use for Sunday school. The "tree" also provides a visual vehicle to include children in the home on an Advent journey.

Creatively artistic or plain, daily or weekly, you choose. These Scriptures and symbols should of course express the hope and truth that we, as Gentiles, have now become part of the holy lineage of Christ.

Ponder:

Paul, writing in Romans 15:9–12, refers to some Old Testament passages. He quotes,

" 'Therefore I will praise you, O Lord, among the Gentiles; I will sing hymns to your name' [2 Samuel 22:50; Psalm 18:49]. Again, it says. 'Rejoice, O Gentiles, with his people' [Deuteronomy 32:43]. And again, 'Praise the Lord, all you Gentiles, and sing praises to him, all you peoples' [Psalm 117:1]. And again, Isaiah says, 'The Root of Jesse will spring up, one who will arise to rule over the nations; in him the Gentiles will hope' " [Isaiah 11:10].

Dwell:

To us a Child of hope is born,
To us a Son is giv'n,
Him shall the tribes of earth obey,
Him all the hosts of Heav'n.

His Name shall be the Prince of Peace,
Forevermore adorned,
The Wonderful, the Counselor,
The great and mighty Lord.

To us a Child of hope is born,
To us a Son is giv'n,
The Wonderful, the Counselor,
The mighty Lord of Heav'n.[v]

Action:

Jesus is the long awaited Messiah whom God sent to bring salvation to the Jews and the Gentiles. Pray for all Jewish people who have yet to recognize and receive Yeshua—the Christ—the One who has already come.

We have this hope as an anchor for the soul, firm and secure. It enters the inner sanctuary behind the curtain.

HEBREWS 6:19

These words form part of the letter to the Hebrews, former Jews and now followers of Christ. It appears that their passion for and trust in Jesus had begun to wane. Returning to Judaism seemed a real possibility. With words of warning and encouragement the author of Hebrews reminded them of Jesus and all He had done for them. They should not turn back. Rather they should get back on track: mature, embrace hope, run the race of faith, and take heart from the great cloud of witnesses cheering them on.

The Church of Scotland, where I grew up, had, like many other denominations, uniformed organizations. Similar to the Boy Scouts, we had the Boys Brigade, founded by Sir William Alexander Smith in Glasgow on October 4, 1883. From this one "Company" formed in Scotland, the BB has grown into a worldwide movement that has worked with millions of children and young people for well over a century. Both my brothers were proud to be members of the local BB and both enjoyed the badge earning, marching, camping, activities, and service projects.

The uniform served as an essential part of belonging to the BB. My mother always made sure her sons' white stripes on the box hat and their brass badges shone brightly. I think my mother took more pride in the boys' appearance than the boys did. Involvement in church services served as another core value. When all these boys and their leaders proudly marched into church, they created a sacred atmosphere. On these particular Sundays, the congregation would sing the BB anthem:

Will your anchor hold in the storms of life,
When the clouds unfold their wings of strife?
When the strong tides lift, and the cables strain,
Will your anchor drift, or firm remain?

We have an anchor that keeps the soul
Steadfast and sure while the billows roll;
Fastened to the Rock which cannot move,
Grounded firm and deep in the Saviour's love!

An anchor with a cross behind it forms the BB logo. The letter B sits boldly on each side of the cross. The words "Sure and Steadfast" appear proudly on the anchor.

Like the Hebrews, at times we all struggle to keep the faith. Whatever the circumstances, we need renewed hope. Our Scripture for today, and the words of this hymn, written by Priscilla Jane Owens in the mid-nineteenth century, provide the medicine we need.

Ponder:

"Praise be to the God and Father of our Lord Jesus Christ! In his great mercy he has given us new birth into a living hope through the resurrection of Jesus Christ from the dead, and into an inheritance that can never perish, spoil or fade . . . kept in heaven for you, who through faith are shielded by God's power until the coming of the salvation that is ready to be revealed in the last time" (1 Peter 1:3–5).

Dwell:

"Find rest, O my soul, in God alone; my hope comes from him" (Psalm 62:5).

Action:

Is there a situation in your life, or the life of someone you know, that seems hopeless?

Write a prayer of lament to God. Like the psalmist, tell him how you feel. Pour out your heart to Him and ask Him to help you or another find hope.

Day 4 Hope

Why are you downcast, O my soul? Why so disturbed within me? Put your hope in God, for I will yet praise him, my Savior and my God.

PSALM 42:5

These words appear once more in verse 11 and yet again at the end of the following Psalm. This author, the director of music, probably led the worshippers to the temple in Jerusalem. Those days vanished, as did the temple. The sin of the people and their disobedience to God led to their exile in Babylon.

St. Patrick found himself in exile in Ireland. Was it his sin and disobedience to God, or was it just bad luck that when the marauding pirates came to steal and pillage, they captured Patrick and took him to Ireland to sell him as a slave?

Patrick's *Confession*, an autobiography, begins with these words: "I, Patrick a sinner . . ." Section 44 of his Confession reveals that his battle with sin continued beyond the time when he put his hope in Christ and sought to serve his Lord:

So I hope that I did as I ought, but I do not trust myself as long as I am in this mortal body, for he is strong who strives daily to turn me away from the faith and true holiness to which I aspire until the end of my life for Christ my Lord, but the hostile flesh is always dragging one down to death, that is, to unlawful attractions. And I know in part why I did not lead a perfect life like other believers, but I confess to my Lord and do not blush in his sight, because I am not lying; from the time when I came to know him in my youth, the love of God and fear of him increased in me, and right up until now, by God's favour, I have kept the faith.

Discouragement often came to Patrick, as it did to the psalmist. Similar to the Israelites, Patrick struggled with temptations and sin. He knew his need of God and of the forgiveness the Cross provides. He found hope in the saving power of Jesus Christ: a power so great that even in the darkest times he, like the psalmist, turned his downcast heart heavenward with the desire to praise God.

Advent, over the years, has developed into a season of anticipation and hope, but we must always remember that unless we address the sin in our lives, our hope will remain an unattainable dream. Often, sin brings discouragement to our souls, and we become downcast and disturbed. When this happens we can restore our hope through Christ.

1 John 1:8–9 states, "If we claim to be without sin, we deceive ourselves and the truth is not in us. If we confess our sins, he is faithful and just and will forgive us our sins and purify us from all unrighteousness."

"You, O Lord, are a compassionate and gracious God, slow to anger, abounding in love and faithfulness" (Psalm 86:15).

No wonder the psalmist urges us to "put our hope in God."

Ponder:

The ancient Celtic Christians fully embraced Confessional Prayer. St. Patrick's *Confession* highlights this. We, like Patrick, need the forgiving love of God to cleanse us daily.

Dwell:

My hope is built on nothing less than Jesus blood and righteousness;
I dare not trust my sweetest frame, but wholly lean on Jesus' name.
On Christ, the solid rock I stand; all other ground is sinking sand.

His oath, his covenant, and blood, support me in the whelming flood;
When all around my soul gives way, he then is all my hope and stay:
On Christ, the solid rock I stand; all other ground is sinking sand.[vi]

Action:

An anonymous early Irish cry for cleansing put it this way:

Jesus, forgive my sins.
Forgive the sins that I can remember, and also the sins I have forgotten.
Forgive the wrong actions I have committed, and the right actions I have omitted.
Forgive the times I have been weak in the face of temptation, and those when I have been stubborn in the face of correction.
Forgive the times I have been proud of my own achievements, and those when I have failed to boast of your works.
Forgive the harsh judgments I have made of others, and the leniency I have shown myself.
Forgive the lies I have told to others, and the truths I have avoided.
Forgive me of the pain I have caused others, and the indulgence I have shown to myself.
Jesus, have pity on me, and make me whole.

Make this prayer your cry for cleansing this week. May our loving heavenly Father bless and heal as you seek His forgiving grace and the hope found in Him alone.

Be strong and take heart, all you who hope in the Lord.

PSALM 31:24

Hope weaves its "golden" thread throughout the tapestry of Scripture. Often this hope comes in the form of the promise of God's presence with us always.

In Genesis 28:15, we read of God's promise to Jacob. Jacob begins his journey away from all that is familiar. He will face the unknown, but he need not fear. He can leave with hope in his heart and the assurance that he will not travel alone. God says to him, "I am with you and will watch over you wherever you go."

Words of hope and declarations of the Source of such hope fill the Psalms. For example, "Show me your ways, O Lord, teach me your paths; guide me in your truth and teach me, for you are God my Savior, and my hope is in you all day long" (Psalm 25:4–5).

Matthew records Jesus parting words to His disciples as, "And surely I am with you always, to the very end of the age" (28:20). These words, this promise, must have been a source of hope and strength to these disciples in the days, months, and years after Jesus' ascension.

Bill Johnson, in his teaching on Hosting the Presence, calls us as Christians, "Warriors of hope." Warriors of hope? Does that describe you? All too often, when life becomes difficult, fear overwhelms me and I lose sight of hope and forget that He is with me: He is the strength in the midst of my weakness.

The Good News tells us that we can know our God as a God of grace. If we forget He is with us, we don't need to punish ourselves with guilt. Instead, we can give thanks that we remember or, perhaps more accurately, that God reminds us. Psalm 130:3–5 assures us:

If you, O LORD, kept a record of sins,
Lord, who could stand?
But with you there is forgiveness,
so that we can, with reverence, serve you.
I wait for the LORD, my whole being waits,
and in his word I put my hope.

Advent is a time of hope and anticipation. It is a time for remembering how much God loves us. When we do this we banish fear, and we find the strength we need to face whatever comes our way. Paul says, "May the God of hope fill you with all joy and peace as you trust in him, so that you may overflow with hope by the power of the Holy Spirit" (Romans 15:13).

Ponder:

O little town of Bethlehem,
How still we see thee lie!
Above thy deep and dreamless sleep
The silent stars go by:
Yet in the dark streets shineth,
The everlasting Light;
The hopes and fears of all the years
Are met in Thee tonight.[vii]

Dwell:

"Consult not your fears but your hopes and dreams. Think not about your frustrations, but about your unfulfilled potential. Concern yourself not with what you tried and failed in, but with what is still possible for you to do." Pope John XXIII

Action:

What two things do you hope to achieve in the next five years?

1.

2.

Ask God to help you accomplish these goals and to keep a guard on your hope as you wait for their fulfillment.

*Let us hold unswervingly to the hope we profess,
for he who promised is faithful*

HEBREWS 10:23

The hymn "Great Is Thy Faithfulness" will forever remain close to my heart. Laced through the words of this classic worship song, the golden thread of hope has given me new life at times of hopelessness and despair: my first baby born with a major heart defect, his first open heart surgery at eight months; a miscarriage; separation and divorce; loss of my mum. I'm sure you get the picture. You may have a photo gallery of your own times of hopelessness. The separation and divorce left me with the deepest scars.

Having just received communion, the pastor announced this hymn. I don't think I even made it to my feet as the rest of the people stood to sing these wonderful words.

Seated, through tear-filled eyes I read words of hope, a hope I desperately needed:

Great is Thy faithfulness, O God my Father,
There is no shadow of turning with Thee.
Thou changest not, Thy compassions they fail not;
As Thou hast been, Thou forever wilt be.

Was it possible that God, the Almighty and Holy One, would never turn from me? Would He continue to love me and remain faithful to me through thick and thin?

Great is Thy faithfulness! Great is Thy faithfulness!
Morning by morning new mercies I see;
All I have needed Thy hand hath provided;
Great is Thy faithfulness, Lord, unto me!

I had seen His new mercies fall on me before: providing an apartment when we had to leave our home; giving me strength to do the repairs in our new place when all I wanted was sleep; leading me to Scriptures that reminded me I was not alone. All I needed, really needed, He had been providing. The sense of His love wrapping around me like a familiar well-loved blanket caused the tears to flow like a whitewater river.

Pardon for sin and a peace that endureth
Thine own dear presence to cheer and to guide;
Strength for today and bright hope for tomorrow,
Blessings all mine, with ten thousands beside!

"Strength for today and bright hope for tomorrow." I needed that, and here Almighty God, my loving heavenly Father, told me I need not worry. He had all the bases covered. His presence would go with me. He would bless me; comfort me; strengthen me; love me: and give me HOPE. I left the church looking a mess with a swollen and tearstained face, but internally I had grown more whole than I had been for a long time. Hope will do that for us. A hope born out of remembering that our God is faithful.

Ponder:

"But my God shall supply all your need according to his riches in glory by Christ Jesus" (Philippians 4:19 KJV).

Dwell:

Come Thou long expected Jesus,
Born to set Thy people free:
From our fears and sins release us,
Let us find our rest in Thee.
Israel's strength and consolation
Hope of all the earth Thou art;
Dear desire of every nation,
Joy of every longing heart.[viii]

Action:

Give God thanks for the wonderful hope we have through Christ Jesus.

You are my refuge and my shield; I have put my hope in your word.

PSALM 119:114

The ancient Celtic Christians held God's Word in great esteem. Although they had limited access to copies of the biblical stories, their hearts were on fire for Christ. The Celtic scholars and the affluent could read and write, but the majority of the ordinary people remained illiterate. However, these wonderful saints of the past knew the Scriptures. They had an oral tradition that served them well. They memorized passages by heart and one generation taught the next generation.

In our time, Scripture memorization has become a dying art in many churches and families. New and modern approaches to learning have replaced the old system of teaching children the Word. The early Celts in Ireland, Wales, and Scotland had limited options from which to choose. For them, the Word was essential to life. Therefore all people needed it as surely as they needed the air they breathed.

The Celts held the belief that power resided in simply speaking the words of Scripture. Because of their love of nature, they revered the Psalms. They carried the Gospels in their hearts. I suspect that most of us could recite the words of Psalm 23 if called upon to do so, but what about Psalm 119? Yes, Psalm 119, the longest psalm in the Bible: the one with 176 verses. I certainly couldn't recite it. I am good for verse 105 (KJV): "Thy Word is a lamp unto my feet, and a light unto my path." Beyond that, I blank.

Our Celtic brothers and sisters committed Psalm 119 to memory as part of their Christian walk. This served as one of their favorite passages of Scripture. When they spoke it aloud, they experienced the power of the words and found a refuge and a shield in them. They also believed that these words and the words of the Gospels brought healing. When they spoke the Word of God, they did more than recite it. They spoke it as an act of worship, thanksgiving, and adoration.

The Celts learned prayers and poems in the same way. This oral tradition was rich and effective. In the nineteenth century, Alexander Carmichael spent extended time with the people in the western Highlands and Islands of Scotland. He recorded songs, prayers, and blessings, etc., from their oral tradition.

When published by The Scottish Academic Press, he gave it the title, *Carmina Gadelica, Hymns and Incantations Orally Collected in the Highlands and Islands of Scotland and Translated into English*. Thanks to this work we have a greater understanding of the hearts and minds of the Christian Celts, their love of God, and their devotion to His Word.

"I have put my hope in your word." These words reflect the heartbeat of the early Celtic Christian communities. May these same words reflect our heartbeat too.

Ponder:

Regardless of whether you have experienced angels or merely held on to a fraying thread of hope in a time of despair, Jesus cares for you. He will carry you through any situation you face.

Dwell:

All my hope on God is founded,
He doth still my trust renew.
Me through change and chance He guideth,
Only good and only true.
God unknown,
He alone
Calls my heart to be His own.[ix]

Action:

On a score of 1 to 10 where is your current level of hope? In relation to:

Family

Work

Relationship

Faith

Speak to God about each one.

Week Four
Light the **PEACE** Candle

The God of
peace
will soon crush Satan
under your feet.
Romans 16:20

If it is possible, as far as it depends on you, live at peace with everyone.

ROMANS 12:18

As Paul traveled, he constantly kept in touch with the churches he had established. Writing to the church in Rome, he emphasizes God's gift of righteousness and the benefits of Christ's sacrifice. Paul then calls them to respond to all God has done for them: His grace, His mercy, and of course His love.

In Romans chapter twelve, Paul urges his readers to love. "Love must be sincere. Hate what is evil; cling to what is good. Be devoted to one another in love. Honor one another above yourselves" (verses 9-10). He then highlights the importance of remaining joyful in hope, patient in affliction, and faithful in prayer. The exhortations continue. "Bless those who persecute you; bless and do not curse. . . . Do not repay anyone evil for evil" (verses 14, 17). Finally he sums it up in these words, "If it is possible, as far as it depends on you, live at peace with everyone."

Live at peace with everyone? What about the abusers, the adulterers, the bullies, the rapists, the thieves, the liars, the drug dealers, and the murderers? How can we live at peace with these people? In the movie *Miss Congeniality*, Sandra Bullock plays the part of an undercover FBI agent in the Miss United States beauty pageant. Bullock, as a contestant, reaches the final five.

The host asks each of the finalists a question with regard to what our society needs. To the applause of the audience, the first four give the stock answer, "World peace." Bullock's character boldly lists several things that society needs to put right. A stunned silence ensues. Then she gives the longed for answer: "world peace."

Hate what is evil and cling to what is good is well within our human capacity. Blessing those who persecute us and not repaying evil for evil is another story. Paul's grace to us comes in the two phrases before the words "Live at peace with everyone": "If it is possible" and "as far as it depends on you." These provide us with loopholes. In our human nature it seems impossible for us to live at peace with those who have hurt us or those whom we love. Why would we even want to do this? They have inflicted wounds. Pain permeates depth of our being. Yet, Paul urges us to live at peace with our offenders.

Eleanor Roosevelt said, "It isn't enough to talk about peace. One must believe in it. And it isn't enough to believe in it. One must work at it."

If we depend on our human nature, our human strength, our human love, or our human capacity to forgive, our list of those with whom we can live at peace will become short, very short. Our nature seeks revenge, holds a grudge, and clings to bitterness. In this way of living, peace becomes illusive. We find ourselves longing for the very thing our un-forgiveness eliminates.

Forgiveness seems extremely difficult at times, but it remains essential to finding peace. The good news is it doesn't depend solely on us. God can fill us with the grace and love we need to do the impossible. He knows the cost of forgiveness. He gave His Son, the Prince of Peace, that we may know peace. With God's help, we can live at peace with more people than we can imagine.

Ponder:

Are there people in your life with whom you struggle to live at peace? You may want to make a list.

Dwell:

"God demonstrates his own love for us in this: "While we were still sinners, Christ died for us" (Romans 5:8).

Action:

"Peace is a journey of a thousand miles and it must be taken one step at a time." Lyndon B. Johnson

Many, if not all, of these steps will have the word *forgive* on it. Invite God to fill you with His mercy, love, and grace. As He does so, take some steps, even just one, on this journey to peace. You will find freedom as you forgive those who have hurt you, and with that freedom you will find peace.

But he was pierced for our transgressions, he was crushed for our iniquities; the punishment that brought us peace was on him, and by his wounds we are healed.

ISAIAH 53:5

Peace often eludes one who has a troubled heart. A sense of desperation floods our being, and we long for the storm to grow calm. These storms come in all shapes and sizes, but the heartfelt cry of those in the midst of it remains the same: *"Lord, save us!"*

Richard Gibbons, the professor of evangelism at Glasgow Bible College, made his announcement. The annual Glasgow City Mission banquet was taking place the following week, and he requested that two students attend to give their testimony. His words struck a deep place in my heart. This presented an opportunity to give glory to God. I signed up. I looked forward to the event. What a privilege to speak about my Savior. Marisa, my fellow student, also agreed to attend. It would be a great night.

The day of the banquet arrived. Richard scheduled a short meeting with Marisa and me. He went over the details of the night: time, place, order of speaking, etc. Then he dropped the bombshell. Marisa would give her testimony, and I would now speak about why I attended the Bible College. Ordinarily, this would have been a breeze, but not that day. My heart, mind, soul, and spirit became consumed by the storm this change had caused.

I could give my personal testimony about coming to Christ, but speak about why I was at the Bible college: not a chance.

Did I say any of this out loud?

No, I smiled and accepted the change. I gave no hint in my

demeanor that peace had left the building and turbulence driven by anxiety had replaced it. I loved studying at Glasgow Bible College, and I knew God had called me there. Unfortunately, throughout that particular day my mind had spiraled to a different place. Doubt reigned supreme, and I questioned why I ever thought that I should attend Bible College.

Evening came. Richard, Marisa, and I met for prayer. I stayed silent about my dilemma. The event began. Hymns and speakers interspersed. Marisa blessed the people with her testimony. Line by line, the order of the evening progressed. Each passing item increased my anxiety. Panic set in. I prayed that Jesus would come back right there and then. I also considered feigning illness.

Only one more hymn until I would be introduced. I could hardly breathe.

Voices raised in worship sang the first verse of "How Great Thou Art." My silent heart cried, *Lord, take me now*. The storm inside reached its peak. Now we were singing verse three.

And when I think, that God His Son not sparing
Sent Him to die, I scarce could take it in.
That on the cross, my burden gladly bearing
He bled and died to take away my sin.

The storm evaporated. Every part of my being became calm. Anticipation replaced fear. I knew without any shadow of a doubt why I was at Glasgow Bible College. "He was pierced for *my* transgressions, he was crushed for *my* iniquities; the punishment that brought *me* peace was on him, and by his wounds *I* am healed."

Ponder:

"Therefore, since we have been justified through faith, we have peace with God through our Lord Jesus Christ" (Romans 5:1).

Dwell:

"May the God of peace, who through the blood of the eternal covenant brought back from the dead our Lord Jesus, that great Shepherd of the sheep, equip you with everything good for doing his will, and may he work in us what is pleasing to him, through Jesus Christ, to whom be glory for ever and ever. Amen" (Hebrews 13:20–21).

Action:

In Mark's account of Jesus out in the water with the disciples in the midst of a storm, the disciples look to Jesus for help. Jesus says to the wind and waves, "Peace be still." All becomes calm.

Sometimes, when we ask Jesus for help in the midst of our storm, the raging wind and the overpowering waves remain. During that time He says to *us*, "Peace be still." Our circumstances may not change, but He calms the storm within.

In such circumstances we can use the following words, as our personal anthem:

When peace, like a river, attendeth my way,
When sorrows like sea billows roll;
Whatever my lot, thou hast taught me to say,
It is well; it is well, with my soul.

Though Satan should buffet, though trials should come,
Let this blest assurance control,
That Christ has regarded my helpless estate,
And has shed His own blood for my soul.

It is well with my soul,
It is well; it is well, with my soul.[x]

You will keep in perfect peace those whose minds are steadfast, because they trust in you.

ISAIAH 26:3

St. Patrick's exact birthplace is not known. Tradition sets his birth, possibly in modern day Scotland or Wales, somewhere around AD 389. His father was a deacon and his grandfather a priest in the church, but Patrick had no interest in the things of God.

At the age of sixteen, brigands kidnapped Patrick, took him to Ireland, and sold him as a slave. His master was harsh. The life of luxury Patrick once enjoyed became a distant memory. Out in the open fields, in all kinds of weather, Patrick looked after his master's sheep. All home comforts disappeared, and with them, all the talk of God he had grown up hearing. The Scriptures he had rejected, along with the teachings he had disdained and ignored, fell silent.

For more than six years, Patrick remained a captive, and during those years, he knew only loneliness as his companion. Fear and distress clothed him, and despair became his daily food. Yet God had not forgotten Patrick but had begun to draw him to Christ. In the midst of the darkness, the light of God's Word came back to Patrick. The very things he had despised became his lifeline. Instead of focusing on his situation, he focused on God. He developed a prayer life and set his heart and mind on the One he had previously disregarded.

In section sixteen of his *Confession*, Patrick states:

But after I reached Ireland I used to pasture the flock each day and I used to pray many times a day. More and more did the love of God, and my fear of him and faith increase, and my spirit was moved so that in a day [I said] from one up to a hundred prayers, and in the night a like number; besides I used to stay out in the forests and on the mountain and I would wake up before daylight to pray in the snow, in icy coldness, in rain, and I used to feel neither ill nor any slothfulness, because, as I now see, the Spirit was burning in me at that time.

Patrick put his trust in God. He fixed his mind on the One he now believed in. The result: Peace, a deep peace that led to prayer and eventual escape.

Ponder:

"And there the Lord opened my mind to an awareness of my unbelief, in order that, even so late, I might remember my transgressions and turn with all my heart to the Lord my God, who had regard for my insignificance and pitied my youth and ignorance. As he watched over me before I knew him, and before I learned sense or even distinguished between good and evil, he protected me, and consoled me as a father would his son."[xi]

Dwell:

Deep peace of the running wave to you.
Deep peace of the flowing air to you.
Deep peace of the quiet earth to you.
Deep peace to you.
Deep peace of the shining stars to you.
Deep peace of the gentle night to you.
Deep peace of the Prince of Peace to you,
Deep peace to you.[xii]

Action:

The ancient Celts knew hardship, hostilities, and spiritual warfare. Trust in God and keeping their minds steadfast toward the One in whom they found peace served as their main mode of combat.

Write a prayer that reflects your decision to trust God and keep your mind steadfast on Him.

Today Lord, I resolve to:

Peace I leave with you; my peace I give you.
I do not give to you as the world gives.
Do not let your hearts be troubled and do not be afraid.

JOHN 14:27

Preparing children for major change helps them adjust to a new situation. Recently, I observed my son and daughter-in-law doing this for their six-year-old little boy. Life as Nathan knew it soon would change dramatically. The family would move to a new house. As this little one visited possible properties, he indicated his desire to continue living in their current home. Patiently his parents spoke about the positive aspects of the move. Nathan's concerns began to disappear, but the house move was not the only change on the horizon.

Four months after moving into the new house Nathan received the news that he would need to attend a different school. "It will break my heart if I never see my friends again," he said sadly. More words of careful reassurance brought a sense of excitement at the thought of all the new friendships that awaited him. Then another change took the whole family by surprise. A new little member of the family would be arriving in the spring. Nathan initially responded with a good measure of caution but soon, through his parent's words of encouragement and excitement, he came to a place of peace and happiness.

When the time drew near for Jesus to leave His disciples He began to prepare their hearts and minds. Like a loving parent, He sought to comfort and support them. He desired to give them hope and encouragement and assure them of the blessing this change would bring. In verse one of John 14 the first thing Jesus says is, "Do not let your hearts be troubled. Trust in God, trust also in me." He then outlined some of the major changes that would take place. He assured them they would not be alone. He told them the Father would send them another Counselor to be with them forever.

To underline His promise He said, "All this I have spoken while still with you. But the Counselor, the Holy Spirit, whom the Father will send in my name, will teach you all things and will remind you of everything I have said to you" (verses 25-26). Jesus would no longer be with them, but they would not be alone. Although physically absent from them, they would still receive His teaching.

I suspect that Jesus sensed their anxiety and fear. His words of reassurance did not immediately calm their hearts or minds. He needed to add something else. "Peace I leave with you; my peace I give you. I do not give to you as the world gives. Do not let your hearts be troubled and do not be afraid" (verse 27).

The disciples' peace would ebb and flow in the weeks, months, and even years to follow, but Jesus fulfilled the promise He made to them. This promise, this peace that Jesus gave to His disciples, He also gives to us. We may not always sense His peace; however, it is always there. We only need to seek His face and listen to His voice, and we will find it.

Ponder:

Jesus offers you this Word today: "Peace I leave with you; my peace I give you. I do not give to you as the world gives. Do not let your hearts be troubled and do not be afraid" (John 14:27).

Dwell:

In the midst of change, Jesus remains constant. He is the same yesterday and today and forever (Hebrews 13:8). Nothing takes Him by surprise. He already walks on the road ahead of you. There is no need to fear.

Action:

Life always changes, and often the new leaves us with longing for the old. When this happens, we rob ourselves of what Jesus has for us. C.S. Lewis said, "Getting over a painful experience is much like crossing monkey bars. You have to let go at some point in order to move forward."

Ask the Holy Spirit to bring to mind anything you need to let go of in order to fully live in the now and experience Christ's peace?

While they were still talking about this,
Jesus himself stood among them and said to them,
"Peace be with you."

LUKE 24:36

Jesus' birth, so wonderful as it is, needs to be considered alongside His death and resurrection. The baby born in the manger became the man on the cross. Without His death for our sins and the sins of the world, we would face eternity in hell. By God's grace, the good news of the Gospel goes beyond the grave. Satan thought he had defeated the Son of God when His followers placed Jesus in the tomb. They rolled the stone across the entrance and sealed it in place. All could see the signs of the victory of evil.

Fear and despair overcame His followers. How did it all end like this? The peace that Jesus had promised His disciples evaporated. They believed in Jesus as the Messiah, the promised One. They saw His miracles, heard His teachings, and became convinced He was the Son of God. All their hopes, all their faith disappeared when He died on the cross.

But the Prince of Peace would live again.

When things began to go bad, almost all of them disowned Jesus. Even Peter, one of His closest friends, denied even knowing Him. Of the twelve disciples only John remained present when Jesus breathed His last breath.

In human terms, Jesus had every right to bitterness and resentment toward His disciples. When He first appeared to them after the resurrection, He could have spoken words of anger, rebuke, or condemnation. Instead, He lovingly said to them, "Peace be with you."

Despite their faults and failures, despite the fact that they had abandoned Him, despite their inability to remember all He had told them, He thought and desired only to comfort them.

"Peace be with you." Jesus says this to us, as well as His first fickle disciples. "Peace be with you." These remain His words to us, regardless of how faithless and weak we have been. "Peace be with you." These are the words of the Messiah, the One who came as the babe in the manger, the One who died on the cross for our sins, the One who rose victorious over the grave, the One who sits at the right hand of God, and the One who will come again and take us to be with Him forever.

"Peace be with you."

Ponder:

Have you ever denied knowing Jesus? What were the circumstances? Would you do the same again?

Dwell:

No matter how or when we have let Jesus down, His love causes Him to say to us, "Peace be still." Rest in this truth.

Action:

When fear and despair overwhelms us the words of this old hymn by Joseph M. Scriven, written in 1855 can bring comfort and strength, hope and peace. Use them as a prayer today.

What a friend we have in Jesus,
All our sins and grief to bear!
What a privilege to carry
Everything to God in prayer!
O what peace we often forfeit,
O what needless pain we bear,
All because we do not carry
Everything to God in prayer!

Grace and peace to you from God our Father and the Lord Jesus Christ.

1 Corinthians. 1:3

These words form Paul's introductory greeting in his letters to the churches in Rome, Corinth, Galatia, Ephesus, Philippi, Colossae, and Thessalonica. It is also, more or less, his greeting in the personal letters he wrote to Timothy, Titus, and Philemon.

"Grace and peace to you . . ." This repetitive form may cause us to think of these as mere words, an empty pious sentiment, flowing thoughtlessly from the quill of one whom many revered—nothing more than an effective way to win the hearts of his readers.

Grace and peace. It seems that Paul saw these words and their meanings as inseparable. They belonged together like salt and pepper, fish and chips, or mashed potatoes and gravy. If we do not know Paul's story we may believe that his opening words had no depth or personal attachment.

In Paul's heart and mind these words belonged together because he knew of their truth in his own life. He lived these words. They served as his signature at the beginning of his letters, equally important as his name. Paul knew his past well, a past in which even his name had changed. As Saul, he had served as an accomplice in the stoning of Stephen. Saul persecuted Christians and fought against God's kingdom. He sought to destroy Christianity. Yet, despite the evil and sin in his life, despite the fact that he was on his way to imprison more of God's people, Christ met him on the road to Damascus and confronted him with grace.

The details of Saul's amazing conversion appear in Acts 9. Verse 31 of this chapter says, "Then the church throughout Judea, Galilee and

Samaria enjoyed a time of peace." Paul's conversion brought peace to the churches, but equally important it brought peace to Paul himself. Paul knew firsthand that grace provided the pathway to peace, and he longed for all God's people to grasp this. Therefore, he had no better statement with which to open his letters.

Many of us fall into the trap of seeking to earn God's grace. We feel we will never be good enough, and so we attempt to work our way into God's good graces. Legalism has a way of deceiving us. It tricks us into believing that if we do not perform 100 percent God will stop loving us. I lived this way for more years than I wish to remember. Fear would overwhelm me, so I would add more Bible studies, longer quiet times, and deeper prayer times, all in the hope that I would please God and win His favor. By His grace He has shown me that I already please Him because I am His daughter.

At this Advent Season we long for peace. We find this peace, the kind that passes all understanding, through receiving God's grace.

Ponder:

God, in His grace, sent His Son, the Prince of Peace, as the babe in the manger and the man on the cross. That is how much He loves you.

Dwell:

Psalm 103:10 tells us "he [God] does not treat us as our sins deserve or repay us according to our iniquities." Saul who by grace became Paul, the apostle, bore testimony to this wonderful truth.

Let the words of this chorus fill you with peace.

Grace, grace, God's grace,
Grace that will pardon and cleanse within;
Grace, grace, God's grace,
Grace that is greater than all our sin.[xiii]

Action:

Are you constantly striving to win God's love? Or, have you something in your life that you feel could not be covered by God's grace? At this wonderful season, God longs for us to know and receive His grace in such a way that His peace follows.

Read Acts 9:1-31 and see God's grace in action, then choose to trade your striving and your fear for His peace.

"I have told you these things, so that in me you may have peace. In this world you will have trouble.
But take heart! I have overcome the world."

JOHN 16:33

It happened three weeks after my mum passed. I was home alone. The thought of a warm, relaxing bath flowed through my mind. Ten minutes, perhaps even twenty, soaking under some frothy bubbles would soothe my heart and calm my mind. The idea transformed into the perfect plan, and the plan was set in motion.

The water was the perfect temperature. The bubbles were sparkling in the light, causing glorious rainbows to dance around as I stepped into the bath. *Luxury, sheer luxury*, I thought as I burrowed under the warm blanket of foam. It was just what I needed. Time to remember and reflect. The days had rushed by after my mum's death, and this was the first time I was able to think without noise and distractions. *Peace, beautiful peace.*

I knew I couldn't linger too long in this state of luxury. The family would be home soon. I began the preparation to leave my indulgent oasis: Just one more minute, and then I'd force myself to step out of this tranquil state. Sitting up, I gave myself a quick wash. The tranquility of the moment dissipated rapidly. My body now demanded my full attention. As quickly as the bubbles were bursting around me, my peace took flight and in its place came fear.

A lump. I found a lump. I wasn't looking for one, but I found one. I wanted only rest and peace, and now that peace had gone. *Dear Lord, I found a lump.* What should I do? Who should I tell? Perhaps it was the fear that made me decide not to tell my children. Perhaps, I thought, if I didn't talk about it out loud it might not be true.

I knew that I needed God's help, but somehow I was too paralyzed to ask. In the end I called two friends. They both promised to pray for me. It was Saturday evening and I assured my confidants I would seek an appointment with a specialist on Monday. Fear consumed my thoughts and sleep evaded me. Daylight was a welcome friend.

On Monday morning I got up and began preparations for the day. I am not sure how much time passed before I noticed something wonderful. Something miraculous. My fear had gone and peace filled my heart: A deep and powerful peace. What happened to my fear? My circumstances had not changed, but my heart, mind, soul, and spirit had.

God heard the prayers of my dear friends. He saw me, His daughter, struggling, and He sent me His peace. What a glorious gift. Now I could face whatever lay ahead. Eventually, I received good news from the doctors. The lump was nothing more than a cyst that needed to be drained.

Jesus warned us, "In this world you will have trouble." Thankfully, He had more to say. "But take heart! I have overcome the world." He established His peace in the midst of my storm. He promises to establish peace in the midst of your storms too.

Ponder:

Philippians 4:6-7 says, "Do not be anxious about anything, but in every situation, by prayer and petition, with thanksgiving, present your requests to God. And the peace of God, which transcends all understanding, will guard your hearts and your minds in Christ Jesus."

Dwell:

If you are currently in the midst of a storm, Jesus is right there with you. He desires to comfort you and to strengthen you. He will wipe your tears and hold you close to His heart. His presence will fill you with His peace.

Action:

Share with Jesus the trouble you are facing. If you feel too distraught to pray, ask others to pray for you.

Perhaps life is going well for you right now, but you know of others who struggle at this time. Take a few moments and lift them up to God

.

Week Five
Light the **JOY** Candle

Bring **joy**
to your servant,
Lord,
for I put my trust in you.
Psalm 86:4

My lips will shout for joy when I sing praise to you —
I whom you have redeemed.

PSALM 71:23

According to the Merriam-Webster dictionary, the word redeem means:

1. To buy back;

2. To free from what distresses or harms as:

   a. To free from captivity by payment or ransom;

   b. To extricate or help overcome something detrimental;

   c. To release from blame or debt;

   d. To free from the consequences of sin.

God has always been in the business of redemption. From the Garden of Eden to the final redemption we read of in Revelation, salvation flows forth.

Many of the psalms attributed to David speak of his gratitude to God. His words of praise and adoration reflect a life that experienced grace, mercy, love, protection, and redemption from the hand of his Maker. Almighty God chose David, a simple shepherd boy, to be king. He redeemed David from a lowly life and raised him to a position of authority and power. This alone would cause praise and shouts of joy.

Almighty God also rescued and redeemed David from the hands of

Saul: another reason to praise his faithful heavenly Father.

Yet the redemption of his sins touched David's heart at the deepest level. David, a man after God's own heart, committed adultery and murder. Rather than admit his guilt, confess, and face the consequences, he covered his tracks. David wanted to move on with his life, but God could not allow him to do so. God sent Nathan the prophet to David. Nathan proceeded to tell him a parable in which injustice had taken place. This injustice paralleled the injustice David had sought to hide.

David declared that the man in Nathan's story must die for his actions and because he had no pity. In that instant, as if God's light of truth split though the skies, Nathan said to David, "You are the man!" After hearing Nathan reiterate his sins and the consequences that would transpire, David said to Nathan, "I have sinned against the Lord." Nathan replied, "The Lord has taken away your sin. You are not going to die." God's redemption came quickly on the heels of David's confession. A redemption that went beyond any other that David had received.

God offers this grace and redemption to everyone. Long after David's time and long after the promises of a Messiah who would come and redeem a broken world, God sent His only Son Jesus as an atoning sacrifice for the sin of all.

Like David, we need to acknowledge our sin before our Holy God. We need to repent and seek God's forgiveness. When we do, God will give us a clean slate. He will wipe away our sins and we, like David, will be able to say, "My lips will shout for joy when I sing praise to you — I, whom you have redeemed."

Ponder:

"For God did not send his Son into the world to condemn the world, but to save the world through him" (John 3:17).

Dwell:

To God be the glory, great things He hath done,
So loved He the world that He gave us His Son,
Who yielded His life an atonement for sin,
And opened the life gate that all may go in.

Praise the Lord, Praise the Lord,
Let the earth hear His voice;
Praise the Lord, Praise the Lord,
Let the people rejoice;
O come to the Father through Jesus, the Son
And give Him the glory, great things He hath done.

O perfect redemption, the purchase of blood!
To every believer the promise of God;
The vilest offender who truly believes,
That moment from Jesus a pardon receives.[xiv]

Action:

Do you remember when you knew for sure that you were redeemed by God, through Jesus Christ? Celebrate. Rejoice. Sing His Praise.

If you do not have the assurance of God's redemption, take time now to receive His extravagant gift. Believe that Jesus is the Son of God and that He died for you. Acknowledge your sin and ask God to forgive you. Now that you have received His forgiveness: Celebrate. Rejoice. Sing His praise.

Please, also contact the author to tell her your good news.

You will go out in joy and be led forth in peace;
the mountains and hills will burst into song before you,
and all the trees of the field will clap their hands.

Isaiah. 55:12

When I lived in Scotland, I often declared that God had placed me in the wrong climate. Cold and wet, gray and cloudy, windy and only occasionally warm—these do not describe my first choice in weather. On the upside, we have a beautiful countryside. Rich green fields adorn the land. Our eyes can feast on magnificent floral arrays that evoke deep pleasure for the senses. Every garden paints a canvas of vibrant colors. Broad-brush strokes, pretty pastel patterns, intricate, and detailed designs, blend perfectly together.

God called our family to Colorado unexpectedly. Moving across the ocean to live in a "strange" land proved somewhat unsettling. Then I discovered that Colorado has three hundred days of sunshine. O the joy that filled my soul. Three hundred days of sunshine, I could cope with that. We moved to Denver in 1997. The warmth and brightness of the sun provide some of my greatest joys. Breckenridge is one of my favorite places. I love to go there to write. Those majestic Rocky Mountains and the beauty of creation fill my soul to overflowing. While visiting there recently, I found myself in what the Celts would call a *"Thin Place."*

The autumn season had arrived, and I stood on the balcony of my room. The aspens displayed various shades of yellow, orange, and red while the mountains towered in the background. I felt that I stood on holy ground. In awe I soaked in the Presence. From somewhere deep in my being the words of an old hymn rose in worship:

For the beauty of the earth, for the beauty of the skies,
For the love, which from our birth, over and around us lies.
Lord of all, to thee we raise this our sacrifice of praise.

For the beauty of each hour, of the day and of the night,
Hill and vale, and tree and flower, sun and moon and stars of light.
Lord of all, to thee we raise this our sacrifice of praise.[xv]

The air was still. Yet, as if in response to the words that I quietly sang, the trees in front of me began to move; those beautiful aspens swayed back and forth. Before my eyes their leaves broke out into praise to their Creator. Under the leadership of the Great Conductor, these radiant trees played a symphony composed to express exaltation to the King.

In that moment I realized I had experienced something that I had only sung before.

And the trees of the fields will clap their hands,
And the trees of the fields will clap their hands,
And the trees of the fields will clap their hands,
And you'll go out with joy.[xvi]

And I did!

Ponder:

Think of a time when you have encountered God through nature. You may want to invite the Holy Spirit to strengthen this memory. What emotions did it invoke?

Dwell:

Allow the joy of this event to well up in your heart, and bask in the creative genius of the Lord.

Action:

Take time, even a moment or two, to notice the trees in your neighborhood, city, or surrounding area. Most of them will have no foliage in this season, but each one carries with it the promise and joy of new leaves next spring. As we approach Christmas with growing anticipation, let the trees you see serve as a reminder of the promise and joy that the Savior's birth fulfilled. As you do, let your praise arise to God.

You make known to me the path of life; you will fill me with joy in your presence, with eternal pleasures at your right hand.

PSALM 16:11

You don't have to be doing spiritual things all of the time for all of the time to be spiritual. I made this statement several years ago in the midst of counseling a young bride-to-be. As I heard these words, I felt as if I had stumbled upon something very valuable and freeing. I stopped to ponder what I had just said and realized God had patiently taught me this truth for almost twenty years.

Today countless Christians struggle with overwhelming feelings of guilt and shame. It becomes their mantra. This guilt and shame comes, not from involvement in some illicit lifestyle, but merely from the pressures of a busy or difficult life. We lose the hope that God will fill us with joy in His presence, especially if we believe we can only find this in quiet and solitude. Oh, if only we could experience His presence as we walk—and sometimes run—down this path of life on which we find ourselves.

Could this notion have some truth in it—that you don't have to be doing spiritual things all of the time for all of the time to be spiritual? The Celtic Christians certainly believed so.

St. Ninian, considered by many as the Celtic Grandfather of Christianity in Scotland, said, "The fruit of study was to perceive the eternal word of God reflected in every plant and insect, in every bird and animal, and in every man and woman." Encountering God's presence in creation seemed as natural as breathing for the Celtic Christians. This ancient poem reveals this truth.

Jesu Who Ought To Be Praised

It were as easy for Jesu to renew the withered tree
As to wither the new were it His will so to do.
Jesu! Jesu! Jesu! Jesu! Meet it were to praise Him.

There is no plant in the ground but is full of His virtue,
There is no form in the strand but is full of His blessing,
Jesu! Jesu! Jesu! Jesu! Meet it were to praise Him.

There is no life in the sea, there is no creature in the river,
There is naught in the firmament, but proclaims His goodness.
Jesu! Jesu! Jesu! Jesu! Meet it were to praise Him.

There is no bird on the wing, there is no star in the sky,
There is nothing beneath the sun, but proclaims His goodness.
Jesu! Jesu! Jesu! Jesu! Meet it were to praise Him.[xvii]

Emmanuel—God with us: We find Him in all of creation. In the midst of our ordinary day, the joy of His presence can fill us. We just need to know to look for Him. May your joy increase as you find Him on your path of life.

Ponder:

A little child may know Our Father's name of 'Love';
'Tis written on the earth below, and on the sky above.

Around me when I look, His handiwork I see;
This world is like a picture book to teach His name to me.

The thousand little flowers within our garden found,
The rainbow and the soft spring showers, and every pleasant sound;

The birds that sweetly sing, the moon that shines at night,
With every tiny living thing rejoicing in the light;

And every star above, set in the deep blue sky,
All tell me that our God is Love, and tell me He is nigh.[xviii]

Dwell:

You don't have to be doing spiritual things all of the time for all of the time to be spiritual. *Truly, you don't.*

Action:

If you don't do so already, begin to look for God in creation. Take note, or journal the what, where, and when of your encounters with Him. Record also the joy you feel as you experience His presence.

But the angel said to them, "Do not be afraid.
I bring you good news of great joy that will be for all the people".

LUKE 2:10

"Do not be afraid." These words do not necessarily eliminate fear. In fact, they more likely may induce a panic attack. "Do not be afraid," indicates that one either already encounters a scary situation or that one soon will enter some terrifying circumstances.

"Do not be afraid." Can you imagine this scene? In the middle of the night darkness abounds, and only sounds of an occasional sheep bleating breaks the silence. Suddenly, an angel of the Lord appeared and the glory of the Lord shone all around. Talk about the people who walked in darkness seeing a great light??? It's hardly surprising that the shepherds responded with terror!

I love this story of these lowly shepherds receiving the good news of the Savior's birth, but it begs the question, "Why would God choose to reveal His plan of salvation to plain old shepherds?"

The answer is beautiful. The shepherds represent the ordinary, average person. God could have chosen any group of people. He chose the poor and lowly.

When I read this story, I actually hear the voice of Linus in my head. Yes, Linus. I have joined countless others who have made Charlie Brown part of our Christmas tradition. Each year Linus blesses my heart as I watch the well-known story unfold. Charlie looks for the meaning of Christmas, but his closest friends provide no help. He expects joy and happiness at this season. Its absence makes him discouraged and downhearted.

In an effort to find his joy, he attempts to direct a Christmas pageant. It fails miserably. A tree, surely that will produce the answer he seeks. His tree is small, pathetic actually. With all hope gone, Charlie asks if anyone knows the meaning of the Christmas season.

This is where Linus steps in and claims he knows the answer. The lights come up, and Linus begins reading the words from the King James Version of Luke 2: 8–14. Here I use the New International Version:

> "And there were shepherds living out in the fields nearby, keeping watch over their flocks at night. An angel of the Lord appeared to them, and the glory of the Lord shone around them, and they were terrified. But the angel said to them, 'Do not be afraid. I bring you good news of great joy that will be for all the people. Today in the town of David a Savior has been born to you; he is Christ the Lord. This will be a sign to you: You will find a baby wrapped in cloths and lying in a manger.' Suddenly a great company of the heavenly host appeared with the angel, praising God and saying, 'Glory to God in the highest, and on earth peace to those on whom his favor rests.' "

Linus concludes his monologue by simply stating that these words are what makes Christmas Christmas.

The great day of celebration draws near. As the momentum of Advent increases, let us set our fears aside and revel in the good news of great joy that a Savior has been born to us and He is Christ the Lord.

Ponder:

Charlie Brown tried many different ways to find the joy he was looking for. He found that joy in the Word of God—in the good news of Christ's birth. And so can we!

Dwell:

While by the sheep we watched at night,
Glad tidings brought an angel bright.
How great our joy! Great our joy!
Joy, joy, joy! Joy, joy, joy!
Praise we the Lord in heaven on high!
Praise we the Lord in heaven on high!

There shall be born, so he did say,
In Bethlehem a child today.
How great our joy! Great our joy!
Joy, joy, joy! Joy, joy, joy!
Praise we the Lord in heaven on high!
Praise we the Lord in heaven on high!

There shall the Child lie in the stall,
This Child who shall redeem us all.
How great our joy! Great our joy!
 Joy, joy, joy! Joy, joy, joy!
Praise we the Lord in heaven on high!
Praise we the Lord in heaven on high!

This gift of God we'll cherish well.
That ever joy our hearts shall fill.
How great our joy! Great our joy!
Joy, joy, joy! Joy, joy, joy!
Praise we the Lord in heaven on high!
Praise we the Lord in heaven on high![xix]

Action:

"*Suddenly* a great company of the heavenly host appeared with the angel, praising God and saying, "Glory to God in the highest, and on earth peace to those on whom his favor rests." (Italics added.)

Have you experienced a "suddenly" moment with God? Did it bring you joy? Recall the effect it had on you and the impact it had on your faith.

Day 5 Joy

Those who sow in tears will reap with songs of joy.

PSALM 126:5

Tears. We shed them when we feel happy, and we shed them when we feel sad. I admit to crying while watching movies. My daughter and I often laugh till we cry. At the birth of each of our grandchildren . . . I cried. When I experience God's grace . . . I cry. Tears have no respect for time or place. I have tried blinking continually when I feel tears about to flow. I pray that my eyelashes will become sentinels, positioned to block any escaping liquid. My lips begin to quiver, the dam bursts, and there I am—a blubbering mess.

In what I used to call my "Dark Years," tears served as my constant companion. By God's grace I remained strong in front of my children, but the tears I shed at other times could have wiped out drought in a hot climate. At least, at the time it seemed that way. People kindly spoke all sorts of words of encouragement over me, but the pain and sorrow of loss would, all too often, win the day.

I remember sitting on the floor crying, while a dear friend sat silently by my side. Ellen's presence gave me comfort.

She didn't need words.

Thirty minutes passed. The tears still flowed, interrupted only by sobs and sighs. Then Ellen spoke. "God collects all our tears in jars in heaven."

Silence returned.

This time I spoke. "I think heaven is about to fall in on us, with all that I have added." A poignant moment ensued. Then we looked at one another and fell about laughing.

I didn't try to be funny, but humor barged in anyway. God's perfect timing brought some much needed comic relief. It defeated sorrow for the moment. Laughter and joy had a temporary victory. As time passed, joy took back its rightful place in my life. Sadness and pain would recur, but not with the same intensity, and not with the same staying power.

I always referred to those years as my "dark years." In my opinion, this perfectly described them. During one of my Doctor of Ministry courses several years later, I learned to rethink this description.

Leadership was the topic, and I assumed that we would focus on current leadership paradigms. I had studied several of these, and I wondered what, if anything, I would learn.

Our God is a God of surprises. Our instructor's focus did not include current leadership paradigms. He placed godly leadership front and center. All the classes emphasized character: God's character and ours. We received an exercise that changed my opinion of those dark years. It also brought a new level of healing. The assignment asked us to break our life down into five or ten year sections. Our task was to look back and see where and when we perceived the presence of God.

You guessed it. God's presence dominated the time I called my dark years. What a revelation. In the hardship of those years I found the presence of the Light of the World even though I couldn't see it at the time. Those who sow in tears will surely reap in joy. This is God's promise to us all. Now I know for sure that these words are true.

Ponder:

"If you are joyful, do not worry about lukewarmness. Joy will shine in your eyes and in your look, in your conversation and in your countenance. You will not be able to hide it because joy overflows." Mother Teresa

Dwell:

"I will lead the blind by ways they have not known, along unfamiliar paths I will guide them; I will turn the darkness into light before them and make the rough places smooth. These are the things I will do; I will not forsake them" (Isaiah 42:16).

Action:

Look back over your life. Create five- or ten-year blocks. Take note of the times you were aware of God's presence. Praise Him for the joy of this knowledge. If you identify times of pain where God appears to be absent talk to Him with your tears.

Consider it pure joy, my brothers and sisters, whenever you face trials of many kinds, because you know that the testing of your faith develops perseverance.

JAMES 1:2–3

Finding joy in the midst of trials can pose a challenge. Although tested faith develops perseverance, it often lacks enough incentive to lift us to the place of joy.

St. Patrick encountered multiple trials, on a daily basis. He preached Christianity in a pagan land. Powerful druids, who controlled this land, sensed that he threatened the respect and admiration they enjoyed. Patrick knew his need of protection—a protection greater than humans could supply. The following four stanzas from St. Patrick's Breastplate Prayer give us insight as to how the early Celts found joy in the mist of trials.

I bind unto myself today
The strong name of the Trinity.
By invocation of the same,
The three in One and One in Three.

I bind this day to me forever,
By power of faith, Christ's incarnation;
His baptism in the Jordan River;
His death on cross for my salvation;
His bursting from the spicèd tomb:
His riding up the heavenly way;
His coming at the day of doom;
I bind unto myself today.

I bind unto myself today
The power of God to hold and lead,
His eye to watch, His might to stay,
His ear to hearken to my need.
The wisdom of my God to teach,
His hand to guide, His shield to ward,
The word of God to give me speech,
His heavenly host to be my guard.

Christ be with me, Christ within me,
Christ before me, Christ beside me,
Christ to win me, Christ to comfort and restore me
Christ beneath me, Christ above me,
Christ in quiet, Christ in danger,
Christ in hearts of all that love me,
Christ in mouth of friend and stranger.[xx]

These words provide one of the keys to perseverance in the midst of difficult times. May we, as we pray them, remember that we do not face trials alone. God—Father, Son, and Holy Spirit walks with us every minute of every day. With Him at our side, we *can* count our trials as pure joy.

Ponder:

"For our struggle is not against flesh and blood, but against the rulers, against the authorities, against the powers of this dark world and against the spiritual forces of evil in the heavenly realms" (Ephesians 6:12).

Dwell:

"Joy is not the absence of suffering. It is the presence of God."— Robert Schuller

Action:

Write out or copy these words from St. Patrick's Breastplate prayer, and keep them with you. When you feel your joy diminishing, read and reread them until God's presence overrules your sense of despair.

For you make me glad by your deeds, O Lᴏʀᴅ;
I sing for joy at the works of your hands.

Psᴀʟᴍ 92:4

We find the place of richest blessings and ultimate joy at the center of God's will. God taught me this the year my mother died. It was May, and she passed away unexpectedly. Although we had an extremely close relationship, the reality that she had gone didn't really register with me. I conducted her graveside service with professionalism and poise.

Shortly after this time, several women asked me to lead a Bible study. My life was full, and my heart answered, *no*, but my mouth promised to pray about it. After several weeks I sensed God instruct me to say, *yes*. I reluctantly agreed. I suggested the ladies pray and ask God what our focus should be. We set our first meeting for September 19.

The reality of my mother's death hit home at the beginning of September. I was devastated. The sense of loss was overwhelming. I was inconsolable, and I cried out to God for comfort and peace.

The evening of the Bible study arrived. We gathered in Patricia's home and discussed which book of the Bible we would study. Everyone agreed on Nehemiah. We shared praises and concerns. I told of my struggle with grief and how it was now dominating my life. Time came for us to pray. Patricia turned off the gentle music that played in the background. We closed our eyes and bowed our heads. The first voice led our prayers.

Immediately, I sensed something strange. A "pillar" of cloud came from behind me. It rose up over me and lingered there. As a Presbyterian this confused and unsettled me. I decided to take a peek to see if anyone else encountered something strange. No, prayer occupied each person. Interrupting the prayer time seemed inappropriate, so I stayed silent.

Prayer ended and everyone chatted as normal . . . everyone, except me. What had taken place? The "cloud" had come from near the CD player. I asked Patricia what she had played before we prayed. "A CD called *King of the Nations*." I asked her if I could look at the case. I thought, *one of the song titles might hold the key to my mystery.* None of them resonated with me. *Perhaps the words of the songs would bring some revelation.* I took out the sleeve and opened it. There was a general picture of people worshipping. I opened the next fold.

All I could do was cry out, "Mummy, Mummy, it's my Mummy." I now had everyone's attention. "It's my Mummy. It's my Mummy," I repeated. The ladies became very concerned. Tears poured down my face.

There, on the inside of the cover of the CD, was a photo of my mum and my son Greig: a photo taken years earlier in Glasgow at Integrity Music's first recording outside of the USA. If I had not agreed to teach the Bible study, I may never have seen that CD cover. I may never have received this much-needed precious gift.

In my grief I had cried out to the Lord for comfort and peace. He heard me and set a plan in place. Receiving His answer required me to live at the center of His will. By His grace I had said, "Yes." Now I rejoiced in the results. That night I felt Him saying to me, "Be at peace, My child, your mum is here in My presence, worshipping Me."

Lord, I sing for joy at the works of Your hand.

Ponder:

"O People of Zion, who live in Jerusalem, you will weep no more. How gracious he will be when you cry for help! As soon as he hears, he will answer you. . . . Whether you turn to the right or the left, your ears will hear a voice behind you, saying, 'This is the way; walk in it' " (Isaiah 30:19, 21).

Dwell:

"Joy is prayer - Joy is strength - Joy is love - Joy is a net of love by which you can catch souls." Mother Teresa

Action:

Make the words of this powerful hymn your prayer today.

Joyful, joyful we adore Thee, God of glory, Lord of love;
Hearts unfold like flowers before Thee, opening to the sun above.
Melt the clouds of sin and sadness; drive the dark of doubt away;
Giver of immortal gladness, fill us with the light of day!

Thou art giving and forgiving, ever blessing, ever blessed,
Wellspring of the joy of living, ocean depth of happy rest!
Thou our Father, Christ our Brother, all who live in love are Thine;
Teach us how to love each other, lift us to the joy divine.[xxi]

Week Six
Light the **LOVE** Candle

Who shall separate us from the
love of Christ?
For I am convinced that neither
death nor life, neither angels nor
demons, neither the present nor
the future, nor any powers,
neither height nor depth, nor
anything else in all creation,
will be able to separate us from
the **love** of God that is in Christ
Jesus our Lord.
Romans 8:35, 38–39

Give thanks to the LORD, for he is good;
his love endures forever.

PSALM 118:1

The phrase, "his love endures forever," appears forty-one times in the Bible. The Old Testament contains all of the occurrences. The Psalms claim thirty-five of these verses. This becomes hardly surprising when we consider that the various writers of the Psalms desired to acknowledge God's love, power, mercy, grace, faithfulness, and forgiveness. Even in times of lament, the psalmist would bring his focus back to the wonder of God's love.

We may find this attitude of faith—always seeing God as good regardless of our circumstances—difficult to maintain. If we are honest, most of us will have at least one or more stories of times when it seemed that God did not do good and His love disappeared.

One of the most powerful stories I have ever come across concerns Corrie ten Boom. Corrie and her family lived in Holland during World War Two. This Christian family protected and hid countless Jews—and others—from the Nazis. A small space behind a false wall in Corrie's bedroom served as a hiding place. In 1944 the Nazis arrested the whole family and sent them to Dutch prisons. Corrie and her sister Betsie eventually went to the notorious Ravensbruck in Germany. The following excerpt from Corrie's book, *He Cares For You,* highlights a conversation with Betsie about the goodness of God and His love.

Often I have heard people say, "How good God is! We prayed that it would not rain for our church picnic, and look at the lovely weather!" Yes, God is good when He sends good weather. But God was also good when He allowed my sister, Betsie, to starve to death before my eyes in a German concentration camp. I remember one occasion when I was very discouraged there. Everything around us was dark, and there was darkness in my heart. I remember telling Betsie that I thought God had forgotten us. "No, Corrie," said Betsie, "He has not forgotten us. Remember His Word: 'For as the heavens are high above the earth, so great is His steadfast love toward those who fear Him.' " Corrie concludes, "There is an ocean of God's love available—there is plenty for everyone. May God grant you never to doubt that victorious love —whatever the circumstances.

Our God is good. Although evil and dreadful things come into our lives, *He always* remains good and His love endures forever. God's plans for us are always for good, but evil exists in the world, and the evil one wreaks havoc right across society. Often, when bad things invade our lives, we begin to doubt that God loves us. The poison doubt brings begins to seep through the very essence of our being like a raging cancer. Before long, the evil one fills our thoughts with lies about the character of God and His very existence.

You can find the best antidote for these lies by looking at the cross of Calvary. Here we see the extent of God's love for you—His love for me—and His love for the whole world. The baby in the manger that we will rejoice over on Christmas Day became the man on the cross. Jesus suffered and died there for our sins so that we may be forgiven and have eternal life. This is the measure of God's love for us: He *gave* His only Son.

Ponder:

"There is an ocean of God's love available—there is plenty for everyone. May God grant you never to doubt that victorious love—whatever the circumstances." Corrie ten Boom

Dwell:

The steadfast love of the LORD never ceases
His mercies never come to an end.
They are new every morning,
Great is Your faithfulness.
(Lamentations 3:22-23 NRSV)

Action:

Take time to absorb God's love for you today. Let the truth of His Word wind its way down deep into the core of your being. If you have trouble sensing His love, ask Him for a fresh revelation today. He will be delighted to oblige.

"For God so loved the world that he gave his one and only Son, that whoever believes in him shall not perish but have eternal life."

JOHN 3:16

These wonderful words constitute one of my most favorite Scriptures. I gravitate to John 3:16 for several reasons:

1. It encapsulates the Gospel in a nutshell.

2. I grew up with these words of tremendous truth. For me, looking back, they seem to perfectly reflect the central belief of the Church of Scotland.

3. This verse gives me a sense of home. When I read it, I experience the notion of putting on my most comfortable, well-worn cozy sweater that wraps itself around my body like a blanket of love.

4. These words make me feel safe and secure in Christ.

When my husband, Rick, and I felt the call to plant a church, we sought God for His plan and design. Along with our son Greig, we specifically asked God to impart to us the name He had chosen for this church. When we perceived that He was telling us to use 316 (Three Sixteen) for our name, joy welled up in my heart. 316: most churches have words for their names, but not ours. God chose 316 for our name. Just 316. I recall thinking, *what a perfect name.*

The name 316 has brought even greater joy than I had thought possible. For instance, when Rick and I opened an account for the church at our local bank, we sat down with the manager. She asked countless questions to garner the information needed for the never-ending forms. Seated in a small section in the public area of the bank, the manager had almost completed all the paperwork. Suddenly she looked up and said, "Does the name 316 stand for something in particular?"

Only God could orchestrate such a wonderful opportunity to unexpectedly share the Gospel in a clearly secular place of business. Over the past three years several unsuspecting inquirers have asked the same question. It has been our privilege to tell each one of God's redeeming love.

According to Genesis 1 and 2, in the beginning God created. He said. He saw. He called. He made. He set. He blessed. He rested. He formed. He planted. He took. He commanded. He brought. He caused.

Here, in John 3:16 we are reminded that He *loved* and He *gave*. He did so because He loves each one of us. This is the message of Advent and Christmas. This is the message of the Gospel every day of the year.

Our God is not, was not, nor will He ever be a passive God. He desired the best for those He first created, and He desires the best for us today. May we allow God to fill us afresh with His love. May we grasp it, and may we let it shine so brightly that those who dwell in Darkness will see and know the Light of His great love.

Ponder:

"For God did not send his Son into the world to condemn the world, but to save the world through him" (John 3:17).

Dwell:

"The greatest happiness of life is the conviction that we are loved; loved for ourselves, or rather, loved in spite of ourselves." Victor Hugo

Action:

Ask God to give you unexpected opportunities to share the good news of John 3:16.

The LORD your God is with you, he is mighty to save.
He will take great delight in you,
he will quiet you with his love,
he will rejoice over you with singing.

ZEPHANIAH 3:17

Zephaniah's words have the ability to calm my heart and fill me with praise. God—the Omnipotent One, the Almighty and Everlasting One, the Righteous and Holy One—is with me; He takes delight in me; He offers to quiet me with His love; and, just in case that is not enough, He has plans to rejoice over me with singing. I could feast on any one of these words for quite some time and remain content. My love account would reach its maximum ceiling merely by dwelling on one. Yet our heavenly Father chooses to pile on His gifts of love.

Like an adoring parent, God looks upon His children, you and me, and we captivate Him. We may sense something of that intense and overwhelming love in the love that most parents have as they hold their newborn baby. The miracle of life, coupled with the awe this little one provokes, fills the new parents with a love so deep they can hardly contain it.

These parents want to communicate to their precious child all the things we read of here in Zephaniah. They want their son or daughter to know that Mom or Dad stands by them and will protect them. They communicate their delight by posting pictures on Facebook and sending text messages to everyone they know. They smile so broadly that, except for the fact that they have ears; the smile would run all the way round their head. When this little one cries, they happily seek to quiet their baby with their love. Before long they are rejoicing over their child "with singing" whatever comes to their heart and mind.

These responses from earthly parents are wonderful, but they change as the baby grows into a toddler, then on to school age. The teenage years virtually guarantee, at times, to lessen the "taking great delight in." The "rejoicing over with singing" dimension of their love comes and goes. Just ask any parent.

The wonder and awestruck love of God that Zephaniah describes here does not rely on our behavior, performance, or age. Zephaniah first spoke these words to God's people Israel, a people who had turned from God and ended up in exile. Now God reminded them of His loving plans. Their future was bright. God would live in their midst and He would save them. The days of sorrow would be gone and He, the Lord, would take great delight in His people; He would quiet them with His love and rejoice over them with singing.

Although Israel had disobeyed God and had abandoned His ways, God still loved them. Their actions did not alter His faithful love toward them. He was their God and they were His people. Therefore, He loved them.

The adoring love that God had for Israel, He has for us. His love never changes. No matter the circumstances, the Lord looks upon us through the lens of His great love. He sees and knows everything about us, yet His love remains the same.

Ponder:

God—the Omnipotent One, the Almighty and Everlasting One, the Righteous and Holy One—is with you; He takes delight in you.

Dwell:

Love came down at Christmas,
Love all lovely, Love Divine;
Love was born at Christmas,
Star and angels gave the sign.

Worship we the Godhead,
Love Incarnate, Love Divine;
Worship we our Jesus:
But wherewith for sacred sign?

Love shall be our token,
Love be yours and love be mine,
Love to God and all men,
Love for plea and gift and sign.[xxii]

Action:

Take time to experience the presence of your heavenly Father. Let Him quiet any fears or anxiety with His love. Ask God to help you hear Him rejoicing over you with singing. This may appear through Christmas music in a store, a worship song on the radio, some Christmas carolers, a memory of a song from your childhood, or countless other ways.

You may wish to journal your experience.

The LORD appeared to us in the past, saying:
"I have loved you with an everlasting love;
I have drawn you with loving-kindness."

JEREMIAH 31:3

My son, Greig, was six when my brother, Bobby, and his wife, Margaret, visited us in Scotland. It had been many years since they had made the long trip from Australia back to their homeland. We had much fun visiting and catching up with each other's lives. Laughter reigned supreme every day. Bobby enjoyed spending time with his nephews, Fraser and Greig, and with his niece, Fiona, and they enjoyed their uncle just as much.

It was after five days that Bobby came to me and said, "If you were to look in the dictionary at the word 'forthright' you would find a picture of Greig." We both laughed, as Bobby's statement was an accurate one. Greig had the ability to be unashamedly honest. He answered questions directly, in a forthright manner. He was never unkind or hurtful, just beautifully honest. He remains the same today.

I would like to suggest that when we look in the dictionary at the word *love* there should be a picture of God.

God is love. His love is constant, strong, and infinite. Our human love is fickle. It runs out quickly, but the One who loves us with an everlasting love continually draws us to Himself with loving-kindness. The Lord, the Mighty One of Israel, could have demanded that His people Israel return to Him. Instead He wooed them back into relationship with Him through gentle love and infinite patience. He does the same for us.

When held in captivity in Ireland, the young boy Patrick experienced God's everlasting love and His loving kindness. St Patrick bears testimony in his *Confession*:

> Therefore be amazed, you great and small who fear God, and you men of God, eloquent speakers, listen and contemplate. Who was it summoned me, a fool, from the midst of those who appear wise and learned in the law and powerful in rhetoric and in all things? Me, truly wretched in this world, he inspired before others that I could be—if I would—such a one who, with fear and reverence, and faithfully, without complaint, would come to the people to whom the love of Christ brought me and gave me in my lifetime, if I should be worthy, to serve them truly and with humility.[xxiii]

Because of God's loving-kindness, Patrick had an enormous impact on Ireland.

> According, therefore, to the measure of one's faith in the Trinity, one should proceed without holding back from danger to make known the gift of God and everlasting consolation, to spread God's name everywhere with confidence and without fear, in order to leave behind, after my death, foundations for my brethren and sons whom I have baptized in the Lord in so many thousands. And I was not worthy, nor was I such that the Lord should grant his humble servant this, that after hardships and such great trials, after captivity, after many years, he should give me so much favour in these people, a thing which in the time of my youth I neither hoped for nor imagined.[xxiv]

God's love toward us is everlasting. Today, in this Advent season, He is drawing us with His loving-kindness. If we are wise, we will run to His open arms, rejoice, and thank Him.

Ponder:

"This is love: not that we loved God, but that He loved us and sent his Son as an atoning sacrifice for our sins" (1 John 4:10).

Dwell:

The love and affection of heaven be to you,
The love and affection of the saints be to you,
The love and affection of the angels be to you,
The love and affection of the sun be to you,
The love and affection of the moon be to you,
Each day and night of your lives,
To keep you from haters, to keep you from harmers,
To keep you from oppressors.[xxv]

Action:

Write a prayer of gratitude to God for His loving-kindness and His everlasting love.

Day 5 Love

December 21

*See what great love the Father has lavished on us,
that we should be called children of God!
And that is what we are!*

1 JOHN 3:1

When the news broke that Queen Elizabeth II and Prince Philip would visit my hometown, Glasgow, excitement overflowed throughout the city and surrounding areas. Driven by the hope of catching a glimpse of the royal couple, my mum anticipated a trip into the city. I agreed to take her, and we set off for George Square where a public "walk about" by the Queen would take place. I'm not too sure how it happened, but we ended up right at the front of the crowd, right against the waist-high barrier.

The time came for the "walk about" and before I knew it, there, just a few feet away from us, stood the Queen. Oh my word. I raised my camera ready to capture the moment when all of a sudden I heard my mother exclaim, "Oh, Philip." As I turned to see why my mum had become so excited, I saw Prince Philip standing two feet from us. My mum was ecstatic. She kept saying how he looked right in her face. They made eye contact! This explains why she omitted the "Prince," and only cried out, "Oh, Philip." She could not have been more delighted. It was an incredible day.

For weeks, probably months, my mother told her story to virtually anyone who would listen. She eagerly shared the news with her sister, my aunt Anna. My aunt, a big fan of Prince Philip, had to listen to how her sister stood within breathing distance of the prince.

My mother and I waited for hours to catch a glimpse of the royal couple. We, like countless others, would have braved any weather, overcome any obstacle just in the hope of getting near enough to see them up close. So much excitement and anticipation had been generated about seeing the Queen and Prince Philip, and I, along with my mother, had jumped on the bandwagon.

How ironic that neither the Queen nor Prince Philip know we exist. They had no idea we were in the crowd. They didn't go home and pass around photographs of us to their friends saying, "Hey, look, this is Jean and her mother. We saw them when we visited Glasgow. They stood right in front of us, and Philip made eye contact with Jean's mum."

God, on the other hand, knows everything about you and me. He knows us by name. He alone reigns as the King of Kings, but He does not keep us, His subjects, at a distance. His love and acceptance reaches beyond all human capacity: a love so rich and deep that He changed our status from believers in Christ to children of God. "Yet to all who did receive him, to those who believed in his name, he gave the right to become children of God—children born not of natural descent, nor of human decision or a husband's will, but born of God" (John 1:12–13).

In our day and age, most people choose the names for their children based on what is popular or to honor a family member. In biblical times, parents gave names to children for a purpose. But God would sometimes change the names of certain people because He had plans for their lives that their names did not reflect. Abram is a good example of this. God changed his name to Abraham because Abram means, "the father is exalted" while Abraham means "father of many nations." This made no sense, as Abram was childless. Yet God had great plans for this man and those plans all came to fruition. His new name, Abraham, portrayed him perfectly.

We are sons and daughters of the Most High. Paul explains that "now if we are children, then we are heirs—heirs of God and co-heirs with Christ" (Romans 8:17). That makes us *royalty*!

God chose to do this for us. We are royal subjects in His Kingdom—this is a measure of how lavish His love is toward us.

Ponder:

"We all feel the pressure of approaching Christmas. The traffic is terrible. You can't find a parking space. . . . The stores are crowded. . . . Mob scenes make shopping a nightmare. You think about presents— wondering what in the world you can get for so-and-so. You think of friends and loved ones who are so hard to shop for. You can't think of anything they need (which is rather strange when you take time to think of it).

Maybe there is nothing in a store that they need. But what about some token of love—what about love itself . . . and friendship . . . and understanding . . . and consideration . . . and a helping hand . . . and a smile . . . and a prayer?

You can't buy these in any store, and those are the very things people need. We all need them. . . . Blessed will they be who receive them this Christmas or at any time."[xxvi]

Dwell:

Lord, please forgive us for being more excited about earthly things and people than about Your Son. Increase in us a desire to spend more time waiting on the King of Kings with the hope and anticipation of catching a glimpse of Him. Amen.

Action:

You are a child of the King. List four ways that you live, or will choose to live, to reflect your royal heritage.

1.

2.

3.

4.

" 'Love the Lord your God with all your heart and with all your soul and with all your mind and with all your strength.' The second is this: 'Love your neighbor as yourself.' There is no commandment greater than these."

MARK 12:30–31

These words of Jesus, recorded by Mark, came in response to a question posed by one of the teachers of the law, "Of all the commandments, which is the most important?" (Mark 12:28). Jesus responded with speed and clarity, "Love the Lord your God and love your neighbor as yourself." To hammer His response home, Jesus added, "There is no commandment greater than these."

Jesus chooses two commands that summarize the Ten Commandments; the first five commands focus on how to love God, and the second five focus on how to love your neighbor. The first of these two commands, which Jesus elevates above all others, occurs in Deuteronomy 6:5: "Love the LORD your God with all your heart and with all your soul and with all your strength."

The second comes from Leviticus 19:18: "Love your neighbor as yourself."

This three-chord strand of faith, according to Jesus, highlights its ultimate importance: love God, love your neighbor, and love yourself. Over the years I have watched many people struggle deeply with loving themselves. The backgrounds to their battles have varied greatly: abuse, wounding words, unwise personal decisions, and broken hearts, to name a few.

I have prayed with several women who, in their younger life, had undergone an abortion. Without fail, each of these women deeply regretted their decision and struggled with self-hatred. They acknowledged God's forgiveness but could not forgive themselves.

Jesus understood the importance of us loving ourselves. He understood it so well that He included this in His response. The key to self-love lies in understanding how God sees us. It lies in receiving His love for us. You are the apple of God's eye. You are precious in His sight. Receive His love, and use it to help you love the redeemed *you*, for whom Jesus gave His life.

Such Love, pure as the whitest snow
Such love, weeps for the shame I know
Such love, paying the debt I owe
O Jesus, such love.

Such love, stilling my restlessness
Such love, filling my emptiness
Such love, showing me holiness
O Jesus, such love.

Such love, springs from eternity
Such love, streaming through history
Such love, fountain of life to me
O Jesus, such love.[xxvii]

Ponder:

Do you truly love God with *all* your heart, with *all* your soul, with *all* your mind, and with *all* your strength?

Dwell:

Sit with the words of verse three from the hymn "In the Bleak Midwinter."

What can I give Him,
Poor as I am?
If I were a shepherd,
I would bring a lamb;
If I were a wise man,
I would do my part;
Yet what I can I give Him:
Give my heart.[xxviii]

Action:

" 'Love the Lord your God with all your heart and with all your soul and with all your mind and with all your strength.' The second is this: 'Love your neighbor as yourself.' There is no commandment greater than these."

Write or say a prayer of recommitment that reflects your desire to fully embrace these commands.

Surely goodness and love will follow me all the days of my life, and I will dwell in the house of the LORD forever.

PSALM 23:6

The words of Psalm 23 played an important part in my life for as long as I can remember. They hung on the wall above the fireplace, clearly displaying the truth my mum lived by. My siblings and I memorized this psalm as our first scripture. It was hard not to. These words remained front and center every day as we grew up. Long after we all married and left home, Psalm 23 still had pride of place above the fireplace in whatever home mum lived.

The translation of this psalm on the plaque my mum had was the King James Version. Verse 6 said, "Surely goodness and mercy shall follow me all the days of my life: and I shall dwell in the house of the LORD for ever." The word translated mercy in the King James Version is the Hebrew word *hesed. Hesed* refers to God's love that comes through His covenantal loyalty. Therefore this love is a covenantal love—one that will not be broken.

While I was visiting my sister Sylvia in Australia several months before she died, I wanted to make sure she knew God and that she would be eternally saved. From the very first day, I prayed asking God what I should I say to her. Without fail, every time the same answer came, "Tell her I love her." At first this shocked, perhaps even disappointed, me. Why, I could think of a very different script, several in fact; and dare I say, much better scripts.

As I look back now, I can almost see the smile on God's face as I, His little child thought she had a better plan. "Tell her I love her." It didn't seem like much at the time, but I witnessed the power of His words.

Each day I visited Sylvia or talked with her on the phone, God opened up an opportunity for me to tell Sylvia how much He loved her. During our phone calls in the months after I returned to the U.S., I continued to pass on the message God had for her. She would tell me of her prayers of thanksgiving to God each morning when she woke up, her prayers to Him for strength during the day, and her prayers and praise of Him in the evening.

One day she shared with me that she hadn't always made the best decisions in her life. We spoke about the words that our mum always had above the fireplace, and she told me of the peace she felt in the knowledge that God loved and accepted her.

Shortly after she passed away, I read the words of the hymn "The King of Love My Shepherd Is." Verse 3 caused me to recall my conversation with Sylvia:

Perverse and foolish oft I strayed,
But yet in love he sought me,
And on his shoulder gently laid,
And home, rejoicing, brought me.[xxix]

God in His covenantal love sought my sister, and in His grace He took her home rejoicing.

Ponder:

Hesed: covenantal love is the love that God calls us to show to Him and to one another.

Dwell:

We often think that, if people really knew who we are, they would disown us. We make our biggest mistake when we assume that God would do the same. God knows everything about us. Yet, He still loves us and there is nothing we can ever do to make Him love us less. There is also nothing we can ever do to make Him love us more.

Action:

To all God's people Psalm 23 is a psalm of comfort and love. When we embrace the promises within His words we can say with confidence:

I shall not WANT,

I shall not FEAR,

I shall DWELL in the house of the Lord forever.

Use the words of Psalm 23 as a prayer of loving gratitude.

*"Today in the town of David a Savior has been born to you;
he is Christ the Lord."*

LUKE 2:11

There is a Celtic saying that heaven and earth are only three feet apart, but in *thin places* that distance is even smaller. The Celts celebrated God's gift of *thin places*. A *thin place* is one where we sense or experience the presence of God. This can take place in a sacred building, in the beauty of God's creation, or simply any place that God chooses to reveal Himself. When I visited Ireland, the Hill of Tara, Monasterboice, and Croagh Patrick were all *thin places* for me. There on these ancient sites, heaven and earth became one, and I encountered the presence of Emmanuel.

Secular places can become *thin places* too. I was working on a project at a local coffee shop. Christmas carols blessed me as they filled the air. In the midst of the chatter, the brewing coffee, and the orders relayed from the cashier to the barista, this music reminded me of the *greatness* of God: Waiting customers eagerly received the drinks prepared for them; "Hark the herald angels sing glory to the newborn King." A *thin place* indeed. He is Emmanuel God with us, and He loves to surprise us with His *thin places*.

My dear friend Caran lost her mom a couple of years ago, and the family still grieves her loss. Heading into Christmas always emphasizes her mother's absence. Last year she sent me this text about how she experienced God through her daughter's singing lesson.

AJ was assigned a song by her teacher that just so happens to have been one of my Mom's favorite songs. I just pulled up in my car to wait outside of her lesson (the windows to their house are open). She's singing it and I am amazed at God's providence. The song is "Gesu Bambino." Some of the words: "Oh come let us adore Him, Christ the Lord." What else can we say?

I sent a text back to Caran:

O come let us adore Him, indeed. Thanks for the blessing of this story. A *"thin place"* if ever there was one.

"So Joseph also went up from the town of Nazareth in Galilee to Judea, to Bethlehem the town of David, because he belonged to the house and line of David. He went there to register with Mary, who was pledged to be married to him and was expecting a child. While they were there, the time came for the baby to be born, and she gave birth to her firstborn, a son. She wrapped him in cloths and placed him in a manger, because there was no room for them in the inn" (Luke 2:4–7).

This lowly manger exemplifies one of the most important *thin places* the world has ever known. Cradled there, the Savior who is Christ the Lord lay: heaven and earth merging in one insignificant place on earth, with the purpose of giving all people the most significant gift possible.

Ponder:

"Earth's crammed with heaven, and every common bush afire with God: But only he who sees takes off his shoes." Elizabeth Barrett Browning

Dwell:

Gesu Bambino

When blossoms flower e'er 'mid the snows,
Upon a winter night,
Was born the Child, the Christmas Rose,
The King of Love and Light.
The angels sang, the shepherds sang,
The grateful earth rejoiced;
And at his blessed birth the stars
Their exultation voiced..

O come let us adore Him
O come let us adore Him
O come let us adore Him
Christ the Lord.

Again the heart with rapture glows
To greet the holy night,
That gave the world its Christmas Rose,
Its king of Love and Light
Let ev'ry voice acclaim His name,
The grateful chorus swell
From paradise to earth He came
That we with Him might dwell.

O come let us adore him
O come let us adore him
O come let us adore him
Christ the lord.

Action:

This Christmas expect to encounter Emmanuel. Anticipate meeting him in some unexpected *thin places*. Soak in His presence. Linger as long as you can. Then tell others of your wonderful encounter.

Light the **CHRIST**
Candle

Emmanuel:
God with Us
IS
HERE

*For unto us a child is born, to us a son is given,
and the government will be on his shoulders.
And he will be called Wonderful Counselor,
Mighty God, Everlasting Father, Prince of Peace.*

ISAIAH 9:6

The long awaited fulfillment of Isaiah's prophecy had come. What an amazing sight. An angel of the Lord appeared to the shepherds living out in the fields near Bethlehem. The angel brought good news. "Today in the town of David a Savior has been born to you; he is Christ the Lord. This will be a sign to you: You will find a baby wrapped in cloths and lying in a manger" (Luke 2:11–12). A great company of the heavenly host appears with the angel and great rejoicing ensues.

What happens next is inspiring. We read that after the angels leave, the shepherds say to one another, "Let's go to Bethlehem and see this thing that has happened, which the Lord has told us about" (Luke 2:15). And when they went, they found Mary and Joseph, and the baby, who was lying in the manger.

I am astonished by their actions. I think I would have sat with my shepherd friends and talked about what had just happened. I suspect we would have spent an extended time, sharing our individual experience, interrupting one another, and repeating our story time and time again. I think that after we had exhausted our conversation someone may have suggested we should go and check this out at daybreak.

Not these shepherds; they immediately got up *in haste*. Their response was instant. They did not stop to count the cost of leaving the sheep alone. No record emerges of their concerns regarding setting off on a journey in the dead of night. No record appears of any deliberation whatsoever. Hearing the good news that had been told to them, they took off with great speed. The news they heard must have sounded far-fetched, but they go!!!!!

When the shepherds find the baby just as the angels had said, they cannot contain themselves. Verse 17 informs us, "They spread the word concerning what had been told them about this child." What message did the shepherds share? "Today in the town of David a Savior has been born to you; he is Christ the Lord." All of this would have been exciting in itself, but another dimension is added. Verse 18 tells us that *all* who heard it were amazed at what the shepherds told them. (Italics added)

Can you feel the excitement of the shepherds as they tell their story, which is really the story of the Savior who is Christ?

The prophecy regarding the Messiah has been fulfilled. *Emmanuel— God with us* is here. On this wonderful Christmas Day, as we hear afresh the story of the Savior's birth, what will be our response? Will it be euphoric like that of those first shepherds? Will our joy at the news of Christ's birth be as contagious? The Word became flesh and made His dwelling among us. The light now shines in the darkness, and the darkness will not overshadow it. Thanks be to God for the gift of His Son and our Savior, Jesus Christ.

Ponder:

Calvin Miller, writing in *The Christ of Christmas: Readings for Advent,* says, "We must look to Mary's example to know how to deal with the glorious impossibilities of God. Look how she turned the world upside down by making one simple statement…"

Here Calvin Miller refers to Mary's statement, "For nothing is impossible with God" (Luke 1:37).

Dwell:

Hear the sound of people singing,
All the bells are ringing
For the Christmas Child.
In the streets the lights are glowing,
But there is no knowing
Of the Christmas Child.

Oh, let this Child be born in your heart
Oh, let this Child be born in your heart
Tonight, tonight, tonight, tonight.

Will our wars go on forever,
And will peace be never at Christmas time?
If we keep Him in the manger
Then there is no danger
From the Christmas Child.

Oh, let this Child be born in your heart
Oh, let this Child be born in your heart
Tonight, tonight, tonight, tonight.[xxx]

Action:

Whether you are celebrating this glorious day with family and friends, or whether you will spend it alone, remember that, when God decided to send His Son into the world, He was thinking of you.

Spend a little time taking in this truth then rejoice that you are precious in His sight.

Thanksgiving Day

Now, our God,
we give you **thanks**,
and praise your glorious name.
1 Chronicles 29:13

Thanksgiving Day
Fourth Thursday in November

Enter his gates with thanksgiving and his courts with praise; give thanks to him and praise his name.

PSALM 100:4

My first Thanksgiving in the States caused me a cultural crisis. In the midst of the busyness that saturates the weeks leading up to Christmas, a holiday appeared. Not the kind of holiday that gives one a relaxing break, but a holiday that added its own layer of busyness and stress. Inviting twenty-eight people to my first Thanksgiving meal may have skewed my view of this holiday.

In those early years of living in America, I was homesick for Scotland. It came in waves, often gentle lapping waves that tugged at my heartstrings. At other times, this homesickness came as a raging storm that tossed me around like a small helpless vessel unable to cope with the ocean's angry squall. That first Thanksgiving brought homesickness laced with some of the effects of a raging storm.

I realized, eventually, that I was homesick for what "Thanksgiving" looked like to me. In Britain, Thanksgiving comes in the form of a Harvest Thanksgiving worship service. All my years growing up and all the years of my children growing up, we gathered on the Sunday nearest the autumnal equinox with our church families to give thanks.

Glorious autumn flowers adorned the church; red and golden hues radiated throughout the building, while yellow, orange, and brown tones complimented one another and added luster to the sacred canvas. Sheaves of wheat interspersed with beautifully designed harvest breads, filled the chancel.

As the service began, the children of the church, beaming from ear to ear, would process down the center aisle carrying all sorts of produce. The minister would receive their gifts and add them to the array of goods already strategically placed.

This was our time to bring our gift of thanks to God for all His goodness to us. It was also a time to bring our gifts of food, basic toiletries, and items for winter. The poor or elderly in the neighborhood or the Glasgow City Mission received these goods. Throughout the worship service, thanksgiving formed the theme of the prayers, the message, and the hymns. I can still feel the sense of joy and gratitude as we sang the harvest hymn, "We Plough the Fields, and Scatter," The lyrics written by Matthias Claudius in 1782 were later set to music. Here are the words of verse 4:

We thank Thee, then, O Father, for all things bright and good,
The seed-time and the harvest, our life, our health, our food.
Accept the gifts we offer for all Thy love imparts,
And, what Thou most desirest, our humble, thankful hearts.
All good gifts around us are sent from heaven above;
Then thank the Lord, O thank the Lord, for all His love.[xxxi]

This was the Thanksgiving I knew and loved. This was the Thanksgiving I missed. I still miss my Scottish Thanksgiving, but I have assimilated well to our American Thanksgiving Day. Embracing a Celtic Advent provided the key. Journeying with Emmanuel from the middle of November to Christmas Day has kept my heart focused on Him. For that I am grateful.

Ponder:

A man came across the barn where Satan reportedly kept his seeds. Satan had these seeds ready to sow in the human heart. The man noticed that the seeds of discouragement outnumbered all the rest. When questioned, Satan grudgingly admitted that these seeds would not grow in one particular place. The man asked where the seeds would not grow. Satan despondently replied, "In the heart of a grateful man."

Dwell:

Father, never was love so near;
Tender, my deepest wounds to heal.
Precious to me, your gift of love;
For me you gave your only Son

And now thanks be to God
For His gift beyond words,
The Son whom He loved,
No, He did not withhold Him,
But with Him gave everything.
Now He's everything to me.

Jesus, the heart of God revealed.
With us, feeling the pain we feel.
Cut to the heart, wounded for me,
Taking the blame, making me clean.

And now thanks be to God
For His gift beyond words,
The Son whom He loved,
No, He did not withhold Him,
But with Him gave everything.
Now He's everything to me.[xxxii]

Action:

Write a thank-you note to God. Express your gratitude to Him as the Holy Spirit leads.

About the Author.

Jean Mclachlan Hess is a native of Glasgow, Scotland. A graduate of Glasgow University, she received a Doctor of Ministry from Denver Seminary. Jean has ministered nationally and internationally. For the last five years God has given her a passion for Celtic Christianity. The lives of these ancient brothers and sisters captivated her heart and deepened her relationship with all three persons of the Trinity. Keep in touch with Jean at jeanmclachlanhess@gmail.com or visit www.316denver.com to see the latest news at the church she co-pastors with her husband, Rick.

NOTES

[i] Carmina Gadelica II, 167

[ii] Sarah B. Rhodes, 1870.

[iii] Samuel Longfellow, 1864.

[iv] Bede, "The Life of Cuthbert," *Age of Bede* (New York: Penguin, 1965, revised edition, 1988), 59.

[v] Rev. John Morrison (Scottish Minister), 1781.

[vi] Edward Mote, 1797-1874.

[vii] Phillips Brooks, 1835-1893.

[viii] Charles Wesley, 1745.

[ix] Joachim Neander, 1650-1680.

[x] Horatio G. Spafford, 1873.

[xi] St. Patrick, *The Confession of St. Patrick*, Section 2.

[xii] Adapted from an Ancient Gaelic Rune.

[xiii] Julia H. Johnston, 1849-1919.

[xiv] Fanny J. Crosby, 1840-1915.

[xv] Folliott Sandford Pierpoint, 1835-1917.

[xvi] Stuart Dauermann and Steffi Geiser Rubin, "The Trees of the Field," © 1975 Lillenas Publishing Company. (admin. Song Solutions in the U.K.) All rights reserved. Used by permission.

[xvii] Carmina Gadelica I, 14.

[xviii] Jane Eliza Leeson, 1809-1881.

[xix] Traditional German carol.

[xx] St. Patrick's Breastplate.

[xxi] Henry J. van Dyke, 1907.

[xxii] Christina Rossetti, 1830-1894.

[xxiii] St. Patrick, *The Confession of St. Patrick*, Section 13.

[xxiv] Ibid., Sections 14-15.

[xxv] *Carmina Gadelica* III, 209.

[xxvi] Peter Marshall, *Let's Keep Christmas* (NEW YORK: MCGRAW HILL BOOK COMPANY, INC., 1953), 8-9.

[xxvii] Graham Kendrick, "Such Love," © 1988 Make Way Music.

(admin. By Music Services in the Western Hemisphere) All rights reserved. ASCAP Used by permission.

xxviii Christina Rossetti, 1830-1894.

xxix Henry Williams Baker, 1821-1877.

xxx Graham Kendrick, "The Christmas Child," © 1988 Make Way Music. (admin. By Music Services in the Western Hemisphere) All rights reserved. ASCAP Used by permission.

xxxi Matthias Claudius, 1740-1815.

xxxii Graham Kendrick, "Thanks Be to God," © 1988 Make Way Music. (admin. By Music Services in the Western Hemisphere) All rights reserved. ASCAP Used by permission.